ENHANCING STUDENT ENGAGEMENT ON CAMPUS

Arthur Sandeen

University Press of America,® Inc.
Lanham · New York · Oxford

Copyright © 2003 by
University Press of America,® Inc.
4501 Forbes Boulevard
Suite 200
Lanham, Maryland 20706
UPA Acquisitions Department (301) 459-3366

PO Box 317
Oxford
OX2 9RU, UK

Library of Congress Cataloging-in-Publication Data

Sandeen, Arthur, 1938-
Enhancing student engagement on campus /
Arthur Sandeen.
p. cm.

l. College students—United States—Anecdotes. 2. Counseling in higher
education—United States—Anecdotes. 3. Student activities—
United States—Anecdotes I. Title.

LA229.S243 2003 378.1'98—dc21 2003045669 CIP

ISBN 0-7618-2534-7 (paperback : alk. ppr.)

Contents

Observations and Issues

Insight and Inspiration

Preface

I was fortunate to work as a college administrator for 38 years at Michigan State University, Iowa State University, and the University of Florida. I was fortunate because during these years, I knew thousands of students and became a part of their lives and their education. I loved them all!

Working in universities gave me the opportunity to know students very well – where they were from, where they lived, what they did for fun, what their dreams were, what their worries and personal traumas were, and what they believed. The entire campus served as a "classroom," and it was great fun to see students grow and learn as a result of their many experiences.

The thirty-one personal accounts in this book are stories about my close relationships with students – their hopes, their various activities, and their human foibles – over almost four decades. They are intended to provide insight and understanding about the complex and often perplexing ways colleges and universities deal with their students. A college education consists of far more than the credits students earn from their classroom studies; it is the sum total of their experiences. Good educational administrators do not sit in stuffy offices and simply provide services or enforce rules; they are frequently out on the campus, talking and listening to students, and trying to help them with whatever issues they are facing in their lives.

Faculty colleagues and friends outside of higher education often asked me how I could stand being around so many students all the time. They questioned: "Don't you hate being on call 24 hours a day, responding to every imaginable problem? Don't you get tired of dealing with crises all the time?" I did get tired of it, of course, but whenever I did, it often happened that I would receive a thank you note from a student or a grateful phone call from a parent the same day! Hearing that your efforts might have made a difference in the life of a student is among the greatest satisfactions anyone can have. It's what made me stay in college administration for 38 years, and convinced me I had the best job in the world.

I am now teaching in a graduate program in the administration of higher education, and my job is to help prepare men and women become successful leaders in colleges and universities. Students engage in intensive study of finance, law, organizational theory, the psychology of human development, research methodology, and statistical measurement. They are required to pass comprehensive examinations on their course work, and if successful, complete a doctoral dissertation, where they test the efficacy of a selected leadership theory.

When these graduate students complete this program, it is hoped that they will be prepared to be effective leaders in colleges and universities. However, success as a college administrator is not easily quantified, and does lend itself to statistical or financial measurement. Getting to know students well is not about psychological theory, finance, or law; the essence of good college leadership is the heart! The most successful college leaders are those who have a strong compassion for students and sincerely enjoy being part of their lives. In fact, the best college leaders know that a large part of students' growth and learning takes place outside of formal, classroom study. To be an effective administrator requires one to be actively engaged with students and their lives!

It is very difficult to teach about this humane and compassionate component of leadership in traditional graduate courses. Yet, it is one of the most important factors in the success of academic leaders! College and university administrators may understand complex organizations; they may comprehend legal and financial issues; they may be able to describe psychological theories of human development; and they may know how to conduct research on student learning. However, these understandings and skills alone will not make them successful academic leaders. Above all, they must know and understand students – their backgrounds, their aspirations, their personal problems, their real lives. In short, they must understand that each student has a story! Only when these leaders know and become part of many of these student stories, will they really achieve success.

Successful academic leaders understand how students change during college and gain their greatest satisfaction from seeing students grow. They realize that students have very different academic, social, ethnic, religious, and financial backgrounds and that there are many student cultures on any campus. The task for these leaders is to know and understand the lives of students, and to find ways to connect the institution and its various programs effectively with the needs of the students.

While I had great fun writing these short accounts of my actual, hands-on experiences with students, my intent is serious - to demonstrate through these stories how important it is for educational leaders to be close to the lives of students. College students are not just empty bottles to be filled with educational credits; they are complicated, fun loving, talented, confused, effervescent, exasperating, unpredictable human beings – and they deserve the best and most caring attention we can give them.

To the thousands of students it has been my privilege to know, I say "thank you" for a lifetime of friendship. I love you all!

Student Creativity and Antics

Invitations From Students

Just like most Americans, college students form organizations for every imaginable reason. Their institutions encourage them to do this, as most of these student groups provide leadership and service opportunities, allow students to make friends, and help them become contributing members of the academic community. On the large campuses where I worked during my career, there were usually about 450 student organizations each year, representing the political, social, religious, ethnic, artistic, recreational, and academic interests of the student body. Some organizations had been at the campus for many decades, while others lasted only two or three years. Students were free to invent and establish a group for any legal reason, and the student union had professional staff available to help them with their various programs. Each student organization also had a faculty adviser, which helped to improve the out-of-class relationships between faculty and students.

Virtually all of these student groups conduct programs and activities on the campus for their members and for the benefit of others. Student groups sponsor and conduct distinguished speaker programs, popular concerts, political debates, intramural sports, racial awareness workshops, talent shows, jazz festivals, high school recruitment programs, volunteer services, tutoring programs, drug abuse prevention workshops, religious retreats, social events, and hundreds of other activities. Almost every student is involved in at least one student organization, and for some of them, this activity becomes an important part of their college education.

Most colleges and universities include a modest student activity fee as part of tuition, and this money is then the responsibility of the students to distribute to the various student organizations for some of their programs and activities. In most cases, the central student government group assumes this function and the application and allocation process each year becomes a very lively and competitive affair, often taking weeks to complete. While there are always politics involved in the process, the students do a remarkably fine job of distributing these funds. Of course, they are also aware that if they were to act irresponsibly in this regard, they might lose the privilege granted to them! The funds enable student groups to participate in special travel programs, invite paid speakers to the campus, purchase equipment for various student productions, and support other activities deemed by them to benefit the student body.

Throughout the academic year, these student organizations also have special events, such as initiations, parents' weekends, awards banquets, convocations, and conferences. Many of these are quite elaborate and students work very hard to plan and execute them. While the students conduct most of these activities themselves, faculty and administrators are always invited to them, and if they are not present at some of the major annual activities, their absence is clearly noted! Students love their independence, but they also need a good deal of public recognition! I attended literally thousands of student events during my career, sometimes dashing from one to another so as to be seen at perhaps six different events during one evening. While it sounds tedious, it was actually great fun to be with students and to watch them perform. I suspect I was, in effect, a parent substitute for many of the students. Toward the end of my career, the students loved to torment me by referring to me as their "grandfather."

Most formal student events and ceremonies have speakers, who are usually popular members of the faculty, or if the students are lucky, the head football coach or the president. While students are always well intentioned in the invitations they extend to speakers for such occasions, they are not always well organized in their planning or expert in their execution. I spoke at literally hundreds of such events during my career, and here are some examples of some actual invitations I received:

I received this telephone call in my office one afternoon at 5:30. "Hello, is this Dean Sandeen? I am very honored to extend to you an invitation to be our keynote speaker at the annual Student Government banquet *tonight* at 6:30 in the union ballroom. We invited several distinguished leaders to speak, but they were not able to do it, so we thought we would select you. Can you be there tonight?" I was going to the banquet anyway, so of course, I gave the speech.

One day I received a hand written invitation as follows: "Dear Dr. Sandeen: I am pleased to inform you that you have been selected to serve as a judge for the annual North Dormitory talent show next Saturday night from 8:00 p.m. until 1:00 a.m. Our hall council, after some debate, voted 14-9 in favor of you. Please report to the hall ahead of time to make sure you are there in time for the opening act." I was there at 7:55.

I received a phone call in my office one afternoon from a very naïve freshman who probably had been set up by his friends to contact me: "Yes, is this Dean Sandeen? Our fraternity pledge class is being initiated in our back yard at 3:00 a.m. this Saturday, and we would like you there to give a short speech of congratulations. You would talk right after we complete the final round of paddling." I didn't appear for this speech, but I did have an interesting conversation with the young man and the President of his fraternity!

An agricultural student organization and an engineering group had a long and unfriendly rivalry on our campus, and every year, there was a confrontation between these groups, despite our efforts to prevent it. One year, the presidents of the two groups sent me the following written invitation: "Dean Dean Sandeen: Since you are so familiar with our two organizations, we would like to invite you to serve as the official referee for a mud fest football game we will play next Friday night. We'll explain the rules when you get there. Thank you." This mud fest was great fun; both groups were knee deep in muddy water, and none of the injuries sustained were serious. It was a big improvement on what they usually did.

This was a written invitation to speak at a student banquet, recognizing the top student scholars of the year: "Dear Dean Sandeen: I am pleased to ask you to deliver the keynote address at our banquet on April 25 in the union. I have heard you speak before, so please be brief." I was.

Student organizations often hold special weekend events, such as parent's day. I attended dozens of these wonderful programs, and I remember a special invitation I received for one of them: "Dear Dr. Sandeen: Our annual parent's day banquet will be held in the union on Saturday night at 7:00 p.m. We would like you to be the keynote speaker. The charge for the banquet will be $27.00. If your wife comes, it will be $54. Thank you."

I attended the funeral service of a young African American student who had lost his life in a drowning accident. The church in this small town was filled to capacity and of course, it was a very sad and emotional situation. To my great surprise, the minister announced to the congregation, "And now, a special sermon will be presented by the representative of the university, Dr. Sandeen." I spoke, of course –

something people in student affairs are expected to do, without notice, in almost any situation.

This final invitation is still my favorite: "Dear Dean Sandeen: David and I would be honored if you would conduct our wedding ceremony for us in the University Gardens on June 6, right after graduation. You have been very special in our lives." I quickly became certified as a Notary Public, which apparently qualified me to do this. It was beautiful.

Streaking Through College

One of the many fascinating aspects of working with college students is that each generation is absolutely convinced it is the first to engage in some activity. College students have almost no sense of history (They're not sure which came first...World War II or the Peloponnesian War!) and delight in thinking they have just created a new fad. This is true of their clothes, their language, their dances, and even their pranks. Of course, this naïve bliss they enjoy while thinking they are doing something new only increases their enthusiasm for the activity!

Dashing naked across the campus is certainly not new. It's been called "streaking" for at least 50 years, and before it got this wonderfully descriptive name, students and others engaged in this lively activity for centuries. Streakers report that they get a great kick out of shocking their unsuspecting audiences and they also report feeling invigorated by the process itself.

During my many years in higher education, there were three distinct times when streaking appeared. Each time lasted only a couple of weeks, and each time, the students were wildly enthusiastic about it, and convinced they had just invented the most shocking and most creative prank of all time. For reasons unknown to me, streaking was popular in 1958, 1977, and 1993. I don't remember a single instance of this prank during any other year. I have no idea who decided during these years to engage in the activity; it just happened!

Each time I observed this phenomenon, it took various forms. There were "mass streaks," where as many as 1000 men and women would run naked across the campus late at night, apparently convinced there was safety in numbers. There were also "major event streaks," where a few daring students would dash naked across the stage at a large concert. An individual streak was sometimes accomplished when a student raced through a large classroom during a formal lecture. Of course, in this case, the streaker had to be sure where the exit door was – and that it was open, to assure his rapid escape! My favorite form of streaking, which appeared during every generation, was called "strolling." This entailed two elderly people, hand in hand, walking slowly across the campus, absent any clothing. The strollers always won the most applause from onlookers!

Of course, whenever streaking appeared on the campus, there were public officials, religious leaders, and other irate citizens who were convinced such activity signaled the complete moral collapse of society. They also criticized those of us on the campus for not preventing such an outrage, and implored us to apprehend the student rascals and promptly expel them from school. I would always adopt an appropriate Calvinistic public response in such situations, as most of the criticism was vented against me as the person in charge of student affairs. We could do almost nothing to prevent streaking, and we knew it would be gone as a fad very quickly, so we mainly just looked concerned! We took endless teasing from faculty colleagues, who suggested that we were enjoying the human scenery during the late night, mass streaks on campus!

At a varsity basketball game one night in the large campus arena, a male student streaked the crowd by sprinting diagonally across the playing floor. To his great surprise and disappointment, he ran directly into the arms of a waiting campus policeman at the end of his streak. As the policeman escorted him out of the arena, the student acknowledged the wild cheers of the crowd, who obviously admired his audacity. The campus police released the student without charging him with any violation of the law, and referred the student to our judicial affairs office on campus. Someone had taken a picture of this streak in process, and the police had a copy of this photograph, including it in the referral to our office.

The student was crestfallen, of course, about being apprehended. When I met with him, he described with some pride how he had planned this streak, and how disappointed he was in himself for not anticipating the presence of the campus police! He willingly accepted the sanction of conduct probation for his offense, but then issued an impassioned plea to me, saying that he would do almost anything if I would agree to his request. When I asked what it was, he said, "Please, doc - please do not let my girl friend see me naked in this photo!" Of course, I granted his request.

This lively student graduated the next year, and was commissioned an officer in the United States Marine Corps. After a successful 20-year career, including service in Viet Nam, he retired and now is a successful businessman.

He Just Doesn't Test Well

There are almost 4000 colleges and universities in the United States and student enrollment exceeds 15 million. No other country in the world has succeeded in making higher education available on such a massive scale. It is a unique American achievement, one that is closely related to our advancement as a nation. Going to college is part of the American dream, and millions of families begin planning and saving for the education of their children from the day they are born. A college education has become the primary gateway to the future, and most families believe that a college degree is essential to their sons and daughters' success. Moreover, American colleges and universities have become the envy of the world, and almost a half million students from more than 100 countries each year come to the U.S. to study at our institutions of higher education.

There is a general belief among much of the American population that going to one of the "best" colleges increases one's chances of success. This belief is now reinforced each year with the extremely popular *U.S. News & World Report* rankings of the colleges. Despite considerable research evidence that graduates of one college do about as well as graduates of others, and despite the fact that these rankings are often based on reputation, the public apparently believes in the value of the most elite colleges. There is now a thriving academic coaching industry, where for a considerable fee, parents arrange special tutoring for their high school children, in efforts to improve their scores on the Scholastic Assesment Test or the American College Test. All of this is done, of course, to enhance the student's chances of being admitted to one of the most selective colleges.

Among the 4000 colleges and universities in America, only a small percentage are actually selective in their admissions decisions. At many of the institutions, most of the students who apply are admitted. There is, of course, a self-selection factor, as most students are reasonably realistic about their level of academic achievement and their ability to afford the costs of a particular college. Thus, it is somewhat ironic that so much public attention is given to getting into college, when only about 250 colleges out of the 4000 have the luxury of so many applicants that they can be selective. It may be even more ironic that the colleges with the highest tuitions often attract the highest percentage of applicants! Perhaps Americans believe that "if it costs more, it must be better."

Admission to the most selective colleges has become a volatile social and political issue, as affirmative action policies have been scrutinized rigorously by the courts and the public in several states. Most colleges and universities have worked very hard to diversify their student bodies and have achieved considerable success in this regard, due to affirmative action, recruitment, and financial aid. The highly competitive nature of college admissions at selective institutions has created a pressure cooker job for the Director of Admissions. Often caught between conflicting expectations among faculty, alumni, governing board members, coaches, parents, and elected officials, admissions staff are expected each fall to deliver a student body in the right numbers and with the right gender, race, geographical, athletic, financial, and academic combinations to please everyone. When they miss the mark, their jobs are often in jeopardy.

I have been fortunate to work at institutions that attract large numbers of applicants each year. The selection process is always a difficult matter, as there are usually five or six student applicants for each place in the freshman class. Despite rigorous attempts to publicize the criteria by which students are selected (high school grades and test scores), it is inevitable each year that many special appeals are made by parents, legislators, alumni, faculty friends, and the students themselves. The following are examples of some of these appeals I have been presented on behalf of students:

"He's really a good kid, but he just doesn't test well." Translation: This student has a mediocre academic record, and the SAT or ACT exam are identified as the convenient scapegoat to explain his low achievement. This plea is usually accompanied by an effort to discredit the exam.

"She's very bright, but her grades don't reflect her ability." Translation: This student partied on a non-stop basis in high school and got low grades. Her advocate insists that the student just needs a chance to apply herself in an academic setting where she will be adequately challenged.

"He spent a while exploring his life options." Translation: This student got kicked out of high school but eventually graduated from an alternative school. This "sabbatical leave" is turned into an asset by the applicant's advocate, claiming that the experience has made him more mature.

"It was just an isolated, one-time, minor brush with the law." Translation: This student got busted for at least one serious violation of the law. The father of this applicant might argue, "when the car was stolen, my son wasn't the one who had the drugs – it was really just a misunderstanding!"

"This young woman is a bit unconventional, but she is very creative." Translation: This student wears witch's clothes, doesn't take baths, and hasn't lived at home for two years. But, her advocate pleads, "she's very artistic and would be a fine asset to your student body; she makes and sells her own tie-dyed T-shirts."

"This young man comes from a refined and distinguished family." Translation: His parents are very rich. Advocates of such applicants usually make no mention of grades or test scores, as they believe such matters do not apply to them.

"I recognize, of course, that no special consideration can be given, but you certainly do know she is the Governor's daughter." Translation: She's admitted!

"He comes from a poor background and his high school had very few academic resources to encourage student achievement." Translation: This guy is a lousy student, but he is a 260-pound, all-state linebacker, and the football coach wants him badly. This one may end up on the President's desk!

"Her parents, two uncles, and her grandfather are all alumni." Translation: This student has a mediocre academic record and the family is trying to use their influence, because they know she'll never qualify on academic grounds.

"Look, Sandeen, the President of your university, John Tenbrook, is a close friend of mine, and I know he'll admit my daughter if you don't." Translation: The President's real name is Jack Templeton and even if this caller knew the president, his daughter wouldn't stand a chance!

Despite the well-intentioned and rigorous efforts of selective institutions to admit the best students from among their many applicants, predicting how young people will actually perform is far from being an exact science. As the competition to get admitted to selective colleges continues to intensify, advocates for borderline students will, no doubt, become even more creative in their arguments!

Aren't You Somebody?

On large university campuses, most students do not know the names of senior administrators. They do usually know the name of the president, but most of them wouldn't know the president if they met him or her. This, of course, is not a concern of students, as their lives are busy with dozens of more important activities.

Working in student affairs for many years, my name and picture appeared in the student newspaper quite frequently, as I was being criticized for some action, or was simply present at some student event. As a result, my face, if not my name, was fairly well known on campus.

Whenever there was a significant event on the campus, I felt I should be there. I usually didn't do anything of note beyond making a few, brief comments at a banquet or conference, or simply chatting with the students who were conducting the event. As with most faculty and staff, I knew students expected my presence, as it was an indication of support for their activity.

Late one night, I received a phone call from the campus police, informing me of a small fire in one of the residence halls. I lived only a mile from the campus, so I was there in a few minutes, and all of the three hundred residents were already evacuated, and were standing outside the hall, shivering in the cold weather. There was nothing I could do, of course, but along with the residence hall staff, I talked and joked with some of the students, and was glad to learn that no one had been injured and the fire was restricted to one room.

At that time, one of the residents became quite impatient, as he was cold and wanted to return to his room and get back to sleep. He was convinced the firemen and police in charge were moving too slowly and wanted to find someone who could tell them to allow the students to get back in their rooms. He ran up to me, perhaps thinking he had seen my face before somewhere, and blurted out one of the great questions ever asked of me: "Hey, yeah, you....aren't you somebody?"

After recovering from my laughter, I told him that we were all "somebody" and that I worked in student affairs. Apparently my laughter was infectious, as he began laughing himself, and I assured him the firemen and police were doing their best, and he agreed.

For years after hearing about this incident, friends on campus often greeted me with the same question: "Aren't you somebody?" I'm still searching for a creative reply!

We're A Father!

From 1962-65, my wife and I lived in a large, new residence hall, where I served as the Head Resident Adviser for the 1200 men and women students. We were provided with a nice apartment and our meals, which we ate with the students in the large dining facility in the hall. I had a paid student staff of some 25 undergraduate and graduate students, and I was pursuing my own terminal degree during these years as well. Working in this residence hall was excellent professional preparation for me, as the facility was very innovative for its time; there were 12 classrooms, 4 science laboratories, 18 faculty offices, a 250 seat auditorium, and a 25,000 volume library as part of the university's effort to decentralize its teaching and learning program into "cluster colleges." In this position, I was fortunate to work closely with faculty from many disciplines and with students in all aspects of their academic and personal lives. As a result of my experiences in this wonderful residence hall for three years, I was able to move into major administrative responsibilities very early in my career, as there were very few problems I would encounter as a Dean of Students that I had not already dealt with in this large residence hall! After all, with 1200 students, academic facilities, and faculty offices in the hall itself, it was as large as many small colleges!

The hall was six stories high, with one side housing women and the other side housing men. Connecting these wings was the central facility, which included the dining hall, the classrooms, faculty offices, laboratories, and library. Our apartment was located in the central part of the hall on the first floor, where all of the students passed by each day on their way to class or to the dining hall. My hall office adjoined our apartment. Both my wife and I loved being with the students, and almost every night, there were students in our apartment, playing card games, chatting, or enjoying snacks my wife always seemed to have on hand. We developed very close friendships with the students in the hall during those three years – certainly the closest we've ever enjoyed with students. We saw students in the dining hall, in their rooms, in class, in the laundry room, in our apartment, and with their families when they came to campus. These close friendships with students reminded me throughout the rest of my career how piecemeal most student-institutional relationships are. Students are often fortunate to get to know just one faculty member well at large universities; their contacts are usually very brief and largely formal in nature. If colleges and universities could really know their students, understanding how they live, where they are from, and what they believe, the quality of their educational programs could be significantly improved.

The various floors of the residence hall were purposely designed to serve as cohesive units, and were called houses. There were 24 of them, and the students were free to name their houses and develop their own traditions, governance rules, and activities. Competition among the houses was keen, especially in intramural sports. When my wife became pregnant, the students of the hall became very solicitous toward her, and naturally, a lively competition developed among the houses to guess the exact date when the baby would be born. The men and women students were very kind to us, and (I learned later) made sure that noise was kept to a minimum at night so that my wife could get her needed sleep! They also conducted a lottery, trying to see if anyone could guess the name of the new baby. Despite their efforts to get inside information about this matter from us, they were unsuccessful!

When our daughter, Sara, was born, the students displayed a huge sign outside the hall, which proclaimed to the campus, "We're a father!" Their enthusiasm and support were greatly appreciated of course, although this particular phraseology was a bit worrisome! One of the houses presented our daughter with a $100 savings bond and made her an honorary, lifetime member of their organization. The beautiful citation they gave her in 1963 hangs proudly on a wall in her home, 38 years later. Several other houses also presented her with gifts; it was like 1200 students had adopted our new daughter! Obviously, we never had any difficulty finding a baby sitter in the next two years when we went out for the evening!

When our daughter reached her second birthday, I completed my graduate degree and we moved out of the hall and I took another position. She probably had more loving attention paid to her every day by the students in the hall than any child ever had! And, despite lots of pictures we took during those years of her with the students, she doesn't remember a single part of it! The personal visits we still receive from former residents of this residence hall, even though we moved far away to Florida, are among my most enjoyable experiences. On more than one occasion, the sons and daughters of these former hall residents enrolled at the University of Florida, and their proud parents wanted to make sure they met my wife and me. From my perspective, student affairs work just doesn't get any better than this!

Buried Treasure

Alcohol abuse has been the worst enemy of college students for many generations. Excessive drinking is a major factor in poor academic performance, destruction of property, violence, missed classes and exams, and sexual assault. Alcohol abuse is frequently involved in campus disciplinary cases, and it often masks other serious problems that students have during their college years. Students, like so many others in America, sometimes think alcohol will give them the social confidence they lack or soothe their anger, depression, or feelings of inadequacy.

While it is illegal for those under 21 years of age to consume alcohol, this law is perhaps the most overlooked and violated legislation in the country. The great majority of traditional age college students are under 21, and most of them drink. Most colleges and universities work diligently to observe this law and their own regulations on drinking, but few of them have had much success. National studies of student alcohol abuse indicate that most students drink, regardless of age, and that the number of serious abusers of alcohol is increasing.

A great deal of money and effort have been expended by colleges and universities to educate students about alcohol abuse, and several student organizations have been active themselves in these programs. Many of them have been conducted under the sponsorship of campus student health services, and the emphasis has been on good health practices, not punishment or preaching. While these programs are impressive and deserve continued support, there is scant evidence that they have changed student drinking behavior in any substantial way.

It is ironic that the major sponsors of televised college and professional sports events are beer companies. Everywhere young people look, they are deluged with advertisements for alcohol, where attractive young people are depicted as having a wonderful time. No wonder it is difficult for college students to get together for any social or athletic event and not have alcohol as a part of it.

Alcohol abuse is a serious problem in colleges and universities. However, the perception that most students get drunk every weekend is wrong. Some students do drink excessively, but most students do not, and they handle their various academic and personal responsibilities well. I spent a good deal of time with students who were in trouble because of alcohol abuse, attended many student events where alcohol was being consumed, and observed some very creative attempts by students to conceal their illegal drinking activities. Here are some examples:

I was called about a loud party at a campus fraternity house late one night, and when I walked into the house, it was obvious that a good deal of alcohol was being consumed. This was against our rules, but in my conversations with the house president, I was assured that nothing of the sort was happening. He was a diligent young man, and I had known him for a couple of years. While our conversation in the house basement party room continued, one of the fraternity members, obviously unaware of my presence, tapped a new keg of beer, and the hissing sound and spray of beer from the keg permeated the room. The house president looked at me, completely crestfallen. As he attempted to invent an explanation, he noticed that I could not control my laughter. He succumbed to the inevitable as well, and we both enjoyed a long, absurd laugh together. We both recovered, and the next week, the student president didn't argue at all when I informed him the house was placed on conduct probation for the rest of the semester.

When I worked and lived in a large residence hall, we occasionally had to take conduct action against underage students who brought beer into their rooms. We never spied on them or searched their rooms, but we were not naïve about their various efforts to sneak beer into the hall. One evening, my wife and I were walking in the central part of the hall, and we said hello to one of the freshman residents who happened to be in the same area. He was carrying a large grocery bag, and said he had just been to the store to get some snacks for a floor social event. There was nothing unusual about this, of course, but this unlucky student must have panicked when he saw us, as he dropped the large bag, and two six packs of bottled beer fell to the floor, with broken glass and foamy, cold beer everywhere. He looked at me like it was his last day at the university; my wife rescued the poor student by suggesting that he go with her to our hall apartment to get a mop and broom to clean it up. They did this, and after allowing the student to think about this for a couple of days, I talked with him and told him I was taking no formal disciplinary action. I was sure he had already suffered enough!

For generations, students have devised what they think are novel ways of sneaking alcohol into arenas, stadiums, and concerts. Flasks, binoculars concealed as flasks, and plastic bags filled with booze and taped to legs are only a few examples. We had a night football game at our university and in this old stadium, one of the end zones was a nice, sloping grassy area where fans could sit and enjoy the game. By halftime of the game, it was obvious that a group of about 10 students sitting on the grass were having a lively time, and were not paying much attention to the game. When a campus policeman was called to ask them to quiet down a bit, he didn't see any alcohol, which was not allowed in the stadium. He knew they were drinking beer, but there was no evidence of beer cans or bottles in the area. By the end of the game, the students had become every louder, and the vigilant policeman discovered their secret. The night before the game, these same students had entered the stadium and had buried a large keg of beer (packed appropriately in ice) in the ground in the end zone. Thus, when they returned for the game, all they had to do was connect their hose to their buried treasure, and enjoy their beer. In my experience, it stands alone, winning the top prize for student ingenuity!

Creative Student Politics

Colleges and universities encourage their students to engage in a variety of activities, where they can practice and learn about responsibility, decision-making, compromise, and other aspects of democracy. There are often hundreds of student organizations on a single campus, representing the political, social, religious, academic, recreational, and artistic interests of the students.

Most institutions have a modest activity fee charged to all students as part of their tuition, and usually, the major student governing group is given the responsibility of allocating the funds collected to the various student organizations to support their programs, facilities, and projects. The criteria used to allocate these funds is always a matter of some controversy, and of course, some student groups become angry and frustrated when their proposals for the limited available funds are not successful. Most student affairs administrators do not interfere in this lively annual process, feeling that the experiences the students have in handling the allocations and making the decisions are of educational value.

At most institutions, student groups make formal proposals to a student governing body, describing their programs and plans for the year. These proposals are sometimes quite elaborate, with colorful, printed handouts, computer assisted presentations, detailed financial projections, and testimonials about how the group's previous efforts have benefited campus life. Student groups are then subjected to rigorous scrutiny during an open question period and strive to justify their proposals while being critically questioned. The process is quite impressive, and the students work very hard, the process sometimes taking as long as two or three weeks to conclude. The students responsible for the final allocation are frequently subjected to a good deal of public criticism from their peers, especially in the campus newspaper. It is one of the best examples of the democratic process in action among college students.

Watching this process on three campuses for over three decades, I witnessed a great variety of strategies used by students in their efforts to make their proposals convincing. Student groups used humor, drama, campus celebrities, social favors, and even coercion and threat to try to get their requested allocations. Aping the behavior of some of their elders, at times they tried making deals with those responsible for allocating the funds, by promising campus positions and honors for favorable treatment. Most of the time, the process worked well and honestly, and after a good deal of argument, the decisions were accepted and the students moved on to other issues.

The best lesson in creative politics I observed in this allocation process took place about twenty years ago. A group of graduate students who were parents had tried to convince the student governing group for almost three years that a child care center ought to be funded, which would provide good care for their children, and also would give them more free time to complete their degrees at the university. The group, which consisted mainly of women, presented very logical, well developed proposals, detailing the financial support needed for a childcare center. Since virtually all of the elected students on the governing group were younger undergraduates with no children, they were not very sensitive to the needs of these student parents. The proposals for a childcare center, even though very effectively presented, were denied funds each year. The next year, two lively young mothers in the group decided to try a new tactic – they contacted the campus and city newspapers and the local television station, and suggested that they might want to be present at the student governing group meeting on the evening when their proposal would be made. On that night, while two mothers were making their usual, logical proposal for a childcare center, some 25 other student mothers marched into the large meeting room, carrying their babies. They lined up all around the student-governing group, and made sure the reporters and television crews were paying attention to them. Looking directly into the television camera, one of the mothers said, "Do you, as the governing board for this student body, want to deny this beautiful baby the care she deserves?" The allocation body was so struck with the presence of the mothers and their babies (not to mention the media!) that it immediately voted to allocate the necessary funds to start a child care center. Twenty years later, this center is taken for granted on the campus, and has provided excellent support for thousands of student families.

The childcare program was funded, but mainly, the students involved on both sides of this issue learned a great deal about the democratic process!

Misconceptions and Stereotypes

Fraternity Bashing

College social fraternities were first established around the mid-19th century and continue to this day. Founded on lofty academic, civic, and moral ideals, these groups have provided support and friendship for large numbers of young men. On some campuses, fraternities also house and feed many of the male students. While actual membership in college social fraternities has increased in the past 30 years, it has not kept pace with the rapid expansion of higher education, and now, where social fraternities do exist, they usually comprise a relatively small proportion of the student population.

Social fraternities are part of their own national organizations, and only become part of a college or university when there is an ongoing, cooperative relationship between the institution and the national fraternity. The fraternity must agree to be a contributing member of the campus community and to abide by all the rules and regulations of the academic institution, which is its host.

The fraternity houses may be owned by local house corporations, but might be located on college property leased to the fraternity. On some campuses, the institution itself owns the houses and administers them in the same way it does its own residence halls. Even when the fraternity houses are located on private property off the campus, all of these social groups are subject to university rules and regulations, and have no status as campus student organizations without official university recognition. Most institutions require a resident adviser to live in the house, and provide at least one full time professional staff member to advise and assist the fraternities.

The social fraternities are very competitive with each other in intramural sports, social life, membership, and campus politics. As a result, they are among the most visible student organizations on their campuses, and often have an influence in student life out of proportion to their numbers. Most of their national organizations strongly encourage leadership development and community service, and this emphasis has resulted in some impressive achievements.

Long before the popular movie, *Animal House,* many people had stereotypes of college fraternity men as nothing more than mindless, beer guzzling, barbaric abusers of women. The movie, no doubt, contributed to these notions, but fraternities were used to such characterizations. In some cases, of course, criticisms of fraternities were justified, and most student affairs staff have spent considerable time trying to control the behavior of these groups. Alcohol abuse has always been their worst enemy, and is usually the causal factor in hazing problems, destruction of property, and poor house leadership.

It has become quite fashionable for faculty, staff, alumni, and the general public to bash fraternities, ascribing to them every evil deed they can imagine occurring on college campuses. Even though fraternities may comprise only ten percent of the student body, they are often blamed for most of the problems that gain the attention of the public. It was frequently awkward for those of us in student affairs to find ourselves as the sole supporters of fraternities, as these groups have essentially been dismissed by most faculty and academic administrators as antithetical to the educational mission of the institution.

Without being an apologist for the fraternities, I was always irritated that many of the faculty who were most critical of these groups had not even been in one of the houses for the last 20 years! This was also the case with some administrators and community members. While the fraternities were far from perfect, their members were all students at the university, and those of us who worked with them knew that the great majority of them were fine students and good campus citizens. I knew that if the fraternities would invite their most negative faculty critics to their houses for dinner and conversation, some improvement in relationships and perception might take place. There was nothing new about such an idea, of course, but, to gain a fair understanding of students, there is no substitute for face-to-face interaction with them!

In almost every instance where faculty members, academic administrators, or community leaders met and talked in person with students at fraternity houses, their perceptions were changed. Just as important, some of these adults later volunteered their time and special talents to assist these student groups with financial management, membership recruitment, scholastic improvement, or service projects.

Students, whether living in fraternity houses or anywhere else, need, deserve, and appreciate the attention of faculty and staff. Anyone can deride or bash a fraternity for its misdeeds and write these students off as if they were not part of the institution. A more difficult, yet infinitely more satisfying response is to spend some time getting to know them, offering advice, assistance, and support. The fraternities will only be as good as the faculty, staff, and others at the institution expect them to be!

Dealing with a "Radical" Student

The public often had the impression during the late 1960s and early 1970s that the campuses were overrun with daily protests and demonstrations and that virtually all students hated the country and everything associated with the dreaded "establishment." There were demonstrations, of course, and many of the students were very upset about social issues, but on most days (especially in the winter when it was very cold!), students attended their classes as usual, and in their spare time, pursued their own social interests. Major political or military incidents certainly sparked protests, but most of the time, campus life was relatively calm.

The most dramatic reactions, of course, occurred after the tragic killings at Kent State University in May, 1970. Almost all campuses had large and angry protests, and many of them lasted for several days. Some became violent, causing several colleges and universities to cancel classes for the remainder of the semester and to send the students home. Most institutions remained open, however, primarily by showing patience with the students, listening to their concerns, and adjusting their academic and examination schedules.

As soon as the Kent State incident was reported on the news, there was a large demonstration on our central campus, where speaker after speaker harangued the crowd of over 2000 students about the corrupt government, the inept Ohio National Guard, and the amoral Vietnam War. Moreover, they accused their own university of being an evil participant in this conspiracy, as it conducted research financed with Defense Department funds. Each speaker tried to outdo his/her predecessor by advocating various reforms, which usually elicited cheers from the crowd, but resulted in no specific actions.

As with all such mass meetings, I was there, mingling and talking with students as best I could, hoping to understand what was on the students' minds, but mainly trying to show with my presence that someone from the administration was actually paying attention. While I was often included in those vilified by speakers at student demonstrations, I thought so long as I was one of the students' targets, they at least ought to be able to see me and talk with me during the process.

On this day, one of the speakers was a graduating senior, a fine student and the son of a fairly prominent alumnus whom I had met on several occasions. This student was very upset about social injustice and usually could be counted upon to speak at most of the campus rallies against the war. He was usually fairly well informed and expressed himself quite effectively. But today, just after the Kent State tragedy, he lost some of his eloquence. After denouncing President Nixon, the National Guard, and everything else he could list in his allotted five minutes, he screamed into the microphone, "This University sucks; it is a corrupt institution; Sandeen, you g-----fascist pig, get the mother f------ police off this campus before someone gets hurt!" He then left the portable stage to the cheers of the crowd, and another speaker took his place.

About five minutes later, this same young man who had just admonished me from the platform made his way quietly over to the area where I was standing. He was obviously careful so that his fellow students would not see him with me. I knew the young man well, and after finding me, he said, "Oh, hello, Dean Sandeen. It's good to see you. I hope it will not be an inconvenience, but could I come by your office at about 4:00 and pick up those three letters of recommendation you wrote for me for law school?" I grinned and told him that the letters were ready, and I'd be happy to see him later that day.

This young man graduated and then enrolled in a highly respected law school and excelled in his studies. After completing law school, he clerked for a federal judge, and then joined a prestigious law firm in a midwestern city, where he was made a partner only six years later. When he was 42, he was appointed a district judge. In 1992, he jokingly told me that he voted Republican.

This former student and I have maintained a lively friendship and correspondence since he was an undergraduate. I went to his wedding and when his twin daughters were ready for college, he brought them to my office so that we could meet. I assured his daughters that their father had been a model student during his college days! I expect his annual contributions to our alumni fund will continue to grow!

The "Dumb Jock"

Having competed in intercollegiate sports myself, I naturally took an active interest in the various teams at the universities where I worked. Moreover, because of my position, I served on the athletic board for almost 30 years, and was well acquainted with the coaches and others in the athletic department. Most important, I knew many of the students who competed on the university teams, and in several cases, became friends with their families as well.

I was fortunate to be associated with universities who were part of major athletic conferences, so the level of competition in all sports was very high. Intercollegiate athletics, despite some serious flaws, often serve as a unifying force for the university and its many constituencies. No other activity seems to attract so much public attention, and this can become a great asset for the university. Of course, when serious infractions of N.C.A.A. rules occur, the academic reputation and integrity of the institution can be seriously damaged. Perhaps more than in any area of the university, the athletic program is carefully scrutinized by the public and by the media.

Having known hundreds of students who played on varsity teams over many years, I was always annoyed when I read or heard others talk about "dumb jocks", the stereotyped notion that students who participated in intercollegiate sports were stupid, or were not serious students. At each university where I worked, athletes graduated at a higher rate than the total student body, and every year, many of the team grade point averages were higher than the university average. Most college athletes understand the importance of hard work and good time management, and of course, these qualities are very important in academic success. Many of our athletes have gone on to successful careers in the professions, and are among the most loyal of our alumni.

The most volatile issue on campus for all the years I worked in student affairs was racial relations. There were very few physical confrontations; the most serious problems were lack of communication and understanding, which often prevented close friendships from developing. Without any doubt, the best racial relations on campus were those the students developed as members of intercollegiate sports teams. In athletics, team success depends upon cooperation and hard work, and team members trained, practiced, ate, traveled, and lived together. Conflicts were present, of course, but they were dealt with openly and honestly on the team. Some of the best teaching I have seen was conducted daily by the coaches, who often were significant role models in the lives of these young athletes.

While selected athletes were active in other aspects of student life on the campus, such as student government, interest clubs, and service organizations, most of them spent 20 to 30 hours a week engaged in their sport. Besides the physical demands of this activity, this left little time for them to do much more than attend class and study. This could become pure drudgery for some of them, depriving them of access to the social and educational opportunities so readily available to other students. It is the major reason why some athletes, despite their love for their sport, decide not to continue with it.

The most striking change that occurred in intercollegiate sports during my years in higher education was the increased participation by women. It was a great pleasure to be part of institutional efforts to make this happen, despite the financial struggles and the opposition of some men who did not want this change. Seeing women students competing successfully in many sports, and especially, getting to know the athletes themselves, was very rewarding.

The stereotype of the "dumb jock" college athlete continues to persist among some critics, who obviously do not know some of these students I have been privileged to know:

A young woman from a small town came to the university and excelled as a setter on the volleyball team. An outstanding student who was introduced to medicine by a volunteer physician for the athletic department, she became a successful orthopedic surgeon.

A young, African-American football player, who earned his doctorate in educational administration, and is now a highly respected high school principal.

A young male wrestler from a small town, who made himself a national champion and an Olympic gold medal winner through sheer hard work, who earned a Master's Degree and became a national champion college coach himself.

A young female basketball player, who needed tutoring to pass some of her courses during her first two years in college, who became a successful trial attorney.

A young female tennis player who earned a PhD in biochemistry and is now working on a research team for a research university.

A young male track star, who won a conference title in the intermediate hurdles, earned his M.B.A., and was elected to the state legislature.

Getting to know students who are in intercollegiate sports is like getting to know any other group of students; each one is a special person, and stereotypes just do not fit!

They're Just a Bunch of Bums...

Campus protests of the Vietnam War occurred everywhere after the tragic killings at Kent State University in May 1970. Enraged by these protests, President Nixon chose not to soothe the nation's anguish, but rather to inflame it. Referring to the students who demonstrated against U.S. involvement in the war, the President said, "They're just a bunch of bums." Hearing the President say this on national television, of course, only widened the generation gap and reinforced the disdain many college students had for the government.

For those of us who worked with students every day, the assessment made by the President was disheartening. It was a chilling reminder of how out of touch elected leaders can become when they allow themselves to be isolated from the people. In those years, we had endless conversations with students about their political and religious views, and it was alarming to hear their bitterness, resentment, and distrust toward their government. Some faculty and staff were present at many of the campus demonstrations against the war, and of course, I was there in my student affairs role. Some of these protests were large and unruly; most were peaceful and idealistic; none ever involved more than twenty percent of the student body.

As faculty and student affairs staff, most of us felt the most constructive thing we could do during these difficult times was to talk with students, providing them with a open, non-judgmental outlet for their feelings. Thus, we organized "teach-ins", seminars, panel discussions, and debates; but more important, faculty and staff simply took the time to meet individually with students, listening to their concerns, their conflicts, their anguish, and their plans. These conversations were frequent, lengthy, and often emotional. This personal support given to students by faculty and staff during these years, mostly unknown to the public, was probably a major reason so many young people remained in college and did not give up their basic belief in democracy.

The great majority of the students who participated in campus protests against the war were sincere in their beliefs and felt that it was their obligation to express their feelings and opinions. Of course, there were students who were destructive and violent, but their numbers were miniscule. Most of the campus protesters were serious about their studies, and were responsible members of their communities. As the following descriptions of students I knew during those years illustrate, they certainly were anything but "just a bunch of bums."

One afternoon, I followed a group of about 60 students, who marched a mile from the campus to the office of the local draft board. Draft boards, of course, were obvious symbols of the military establishment, and when picketed by student protesters, provided a stage for their actions which might be picked up by the media. The students were convinced that the public was influenced primarily by what they saw on television; thus, they tried to attract media coverage. After about an hour of peaceful picketing outside of the draft board office, five students from the group decided to block the door to the office. The police warned them that they would be arrested in a few minutes if they didn't desist. I walked up to talk with the five students, as I knew one of them well. While talking with them about the consequences of being arrested, the police threw tear gas canisters at the students, and they (and I!) quickly dispersed, coughing and choking. Bill, the student I knew, was a senior, and was planning to go to medical school. I had spent many hours with him, listening to him talk about his professional plans, but also, his feelings of guilt about getting a student deferment from the draft. He introduced me to his parents one weekend, and they were very supportive of him. He had never been in any trouble before, and hadn't planned to block the doorway of the draft board office. Bill was President of the pre-medical student organization and was on the varsity track team. He was not arrested that day, but was very upset. He remained in college, and graduated. He is now a practicing physician, the father of two daughters, and an active leader of his community. He certainly was not a bum!

A young woman student, Nancy, was the elected leader of a campus religious group. She was a history major, and planned to go on to theological school so that she might someday work in a large, inner city church. She was very active in campus demonstrations against the war, and was one of the most gentle and sensitive students I had known. She frequently spoke out against violence and volunteered many hours each week as a tutor in one of the local elementary schools. I knew her very well, as she was also an elected senator in the student government association. During an off campus demonstration one evening, some protesters started throwing rocks at a police car, and she was hit on the head by a police Billy club. The wound required 10 stitches, but she recovered and charges against her were dropped, as she had been a peaceful participant in the demonstration. She went on to theological school, and now is the minister of her own church in midwestern town. She certainly was not a bum!

I met Frank when he was a freshman, as he was a member of the tennis team, and I enjoyed watching the team's matches whenever I could. He was an excellent student, and wanted to become an attorney. He became very disenchanted with the war, and began participating in campus protests against it. His feelings became so intense that his grades declined, and he quit the tennis team in his junior year. He was close to his parents, and had long conversations with them about the war, and what he should do. He took his obligations as a citizen very seriously, but wondered what he would do if he were drafted. He dropped out of college after his junior year, and seven months later, he received his draft notice. Despite his strong feelings against the war, he entered the Army and served for 12 months in Vietnam. He eventually graduated and became an attorney, but to this day, feels the U.S. involvement in the war was wrong. But, he did his duty. He certainly was not a bum!

Jane was a highly intelligent and feisty young student. Liked by everyone who knew her, she enjoyed the theatre, and had roles in several campus plays. She was a regular participant in campus protests, and often was at the microphone, singing and playing her guitar, or doing bitter satires of establishment figures. Few people wanted to debate with her on any social issues, as she was so smart she quickly exposed the holes in their arguments. Most people did not know that her father was a career Naval officer. Despite his military role, he was very understanding of his daughter's views, and she had great love and admiration for her father. Without his patience and tolerance, Nancy would never have graduated. She became a very creative and successful high school teacher, and an elected member of her city commission. She certainly was not a bum!

What The Students Are Thinking

Because college students represent the future, it seems everyone wants to know about them. Whenever I spoke to alumni groups, local service clubs, groups of business leaders, or newspaper reporters, the question was always the same: "what are the students thinking these days?"

It's easy to fall into the label trap when describing students. In the 40 years I worked in student affairs, here are some of the labels authors and reporters used to describe students: beat, silent, hippy, disaffiliated, me, narcissistic, disengaged, uncommitted, radical, hip-hop, generation x or y, organization kid, and millennials. Dozens of books were written about these various characterizations, and many people believed these labels accurately described the students of the time.

While I read these books and learned from them, the various labels given to students never correlated accurately with my day-to-day experience with them. I found it impossible to characterize all students as fitting one label or to suggest that they all had the same views on any issue. I suspect my comments to alumni groups, service clubs, business leaders, and reporters were disappointing over the years, as I refused to acknowledge any of these labels or to describe students as some kind of monolithic group.

I worked at universities with students from almost every religious, economic, political, and social background; moreover, students came from every state in the country and from more than 100 other countries. Pick any topic; pick any belief system; pick any life style; pick any perspective – all were represented in the diverse student body. Trying to give all these students a label was simply impossible! Thus, whenever I was asked, "what are the students thinking these days?" my response was always the same: "which group out of several hundred would you like me to describe?"

Students in any era are individuals; just because they dress alike, participate in similar social activities, enroll in the same courses, or come from the same city does not mean they all fit the same label. During the Vietnam War, the media often gave the impression that all students were caught up in active protests – nothing could have been further from the truth. Student views about the war (and other issues) ranged from the far right to the far left. At other times, students were described as selfish and interested only in their own personal financial advancement – but those of us who worked with them every day knew hundreds of students who volunteered their time to the needy. When various reporters described another student generation as radical, I wondered what students they were talking about, as most students I knew were conservative, moderate, or liberal.

There are literally dozens of student subcultures on most campuses, and even within these relatively tight knit groups, it is difficult to give them labels or to suggest that their members share the same views on any subject. A college sorority may appear to outsiders as a homogeneous group of affluent, socially polished young women who share the same views. But anyone who knows these young women would laugh at such a characterization, as a full range of conservative, moderate, and liberal views, lifestyles, and values are represented in the organization. I used to attend the annual banquet of the Peruvian student organization – a lively group of about 100 students who engaged in recreational and social events together while also sharing their common cultural background. However, it would be ridiculous to suggest that the members of this student group all had the same views on any subject, or that one label would accurately describe them.

At one alumni gathering, some questions from the audience focused on international students. Since at the time, we had a significant increase in the number of Chinese students enrolled on the campus, one question was, "what is the Chinese student organization like?" My serious reply was, "right now, there are five different Chinese student organizations at the university, representing various political, social, and academic interests!"

Assigning labels to student generations perhaps makes interesting reading, but it is misleading, inaccurate, and unfair. Students of all generations are individuals; whatever their backgrounds, their lives are best described one at a time!

Students and Conformity

Every student generation is convinced it is the first to discover some radical sounding idea, some new approach to living, or some new way to rebel against the established order. This is one of many characteristics that make undergraduate students so much fun; they are refreshingly naïve, and very determined in their various pursuits as they search to find themselves.

The best professors and deans have recognized this for years, of course, and would not do anything to change it. What could be worse than to inform students that the "new" ideas or activities they have just "discovered" are actually old ones which have been around for decades? Some of the best learning occurs as a result of trial and error, and there is rarely a good substitute for self-discovery. Moreover, students learn very little from being told about the world by their elders; it is when they "invent" and experience life, even when they fail, that they learn the most, especially about themselves.

Students absolutely insist that they are not conformists. It is one of the most consistent and humorous of their several characteristics! Every student generation vigorously claims it does not conform to any rigid standard (like their elders do), and argues that it believes in "individualism." No aspect of their behavior contradicts this assertion more dramatically than their dress.

In the 1930s, almost all male students wore ties to class every day, and many wore suits and hats. Women students wore dresses. Shoes were shined; socks and stockings were always worn. Men's hairstyles were neat and trim; women's' were almost always short and rarely touched the shoulders. To deviate from any of these standards would bring instant and unwelcome attention to any student daring enough to try!

After World War II, styles became considerably more casual on campus. But, women still wore dresses, or at least, skirts and sweaters. Saddle shoes and white socks were considered essential. Men wore khaki pants, neat shirts, and sweaters, sometimes with a tie. They also wore saddle shoes or white bucks. Haircuts remained short and neat. While it was obvious that virtually everyone conformed to these standards, most students would have bristled at any suggestion that they were not rugged individualists!

In the 1960s, everything changed – except that students continued to conform! Men and women students let their hair grow long and wore sloppy jeans and coveralls to confirm their disdain for the dreaded establishment. When the weather was warm, they went without shoes, and most of the men tried desperately to grow beards. Going bra-less was expected behavior for women. It was rare to see a tie or a dress, except when these students approached graduation, when there was a mad scramble to "clean up" for a job interview! More than any other generation, the 1960s cadre felt it was highly individualistic; in fact, it was perhaps the most conforming of all!

In the 1970s, male students happily picked up on the psychedelic colors for their "leisure suits" and acted as if those boots they wore were really comfortable. Men cut their hair and actually had it styled to cover their ears and much of their necks. Women began to style their hair again and even wore dresses, although these dresses had to be long and free to swing with the breeze. They were convinced they were part of a new wave….and they all dressed the same!

During the 1980s, someone apparently decided that back packs were necessary to carry books and other items – at all times, for all students, no matter where they were! For generations, students had somehow managed to carry their books under their arms (although men and women always did this differently!), but now, the backpack was ubiquitous. Students all lugged these packs around campus, never imagining that there was any alternative.

In the '90s decade, students continued carrying their backpacks everywhere, but now these packs had become even larger, as there had to be space for their lap top computers. During this time, male students decided to cut their hair short again (and to have cornrows) and women decided to let theirs grow long. Shorts, tank tops, and sandals were the standard in warm weather, and some type of tattoo on some part of one's body seemed necessary. For women students, a cellular telephone affixed permanently to their ear was also standard. But these students, too, insisted that they were not conforming – they were individualists!

It's fun to poke fun at the various conforming behaviors of students. As a faculty member, of course, I do not conform to any of the stereotypes about college professors. Now, if I can just remember what I did with my lecture notes, I will drive my 12 year old Volvo to my class while wearing my tweed sport jacket, my khaki pants, and my L.L. Bean topsiders…..

On the Horns of a Dilemma

Whose Life Is It, Anyway?

Choosing an academic major is frequently a difficult task for many students. Faced with a bewildering number of choices, and often feeling pressures from their peers and family, students are rarely sure they are doing the right thing. Many of them have convinced themselves that their college major will trap them in one career for life, despite an abundance of evidence to the contrary. Some are curious about learning about a new academic field, but are hesitant to take courses related to it because of their fear of failure. This is particularly true, of course, in mathematics and the physical and biological sciences. Others select academic majors because they are more likely to lead to lucrative jobs after graduation, even though they might not be very interested in the field. Most colleges and universities provide excellent career counseling services to address these issues, and strongly encourage their students to use them.

There are many theories of career development which describe the process of selecting a career or college major and offer helpful guidelines and insights to students. Career counselors can provide very useful assistance to students who are trying to decide what it is that they would like to do. But most of these career development theories assume that this process is logical, rational, and sequential in nature; my experience with students clearly indicates that the process of deciding what one wants to do with one's life is rarely any of these! It is usually characterized by changes of mind, emotion, ignorance, frustration, fear, and illusion. Moreover, many students select college majors and professional careers to impress friends and family, or, simply to gain their acceptance or admiration. The process of selecting an academic major and a career accounts for more turmoil in the lives of college students than anything else, with the possible exception of romantic relationships.

A good way to start conversations with students is to ask them to talk about themselves and what it is they would like to do with their lives. Most students respond positively to such invitations from faculty or staff, and of course, contacts like these usually lead to additional conversations about many other issues. This is really the essence of student affairs work, as the relationships students develop with faculty and staff can often lead to new experiences, ideas, and opportunities. While some students may feel uncomfortable having to respond to such questions (or, may even view the process as an intrusion into their private lives), most welcome the opportunity and are sometimes surprised that someone at the university cares about them. In the process of talking about their aspirations and interests, students usually reveal a good deal about their personal backgrounds, their families, and their values. Their stories illustrate how difficult and illogical the career decision process often is and how some of the issues in their lives continue to cause them conflict during their careers.

Jim was young student I knew very well, as he was an active and visible student leader, beginning his sophomore year. He was selected to be a Resident Adviser in a freshman residence hall and then he became the elected president of his fraternity and later, an officer of a service group that provided free tutoring in the local elementary schools. He was an excellent student, majoring in civil engineering, and seemed to enjoy his academic coursework. He had been a successful athlete in high school, and continued his interest in sports in college by playing for various intramural basketball teams. He was a gregarious and popular student and he loved his college leadership and service activities. He seemed to be comfortable talking with me and I became an informal mentor for him during most of his undergraduate years. Jim was from St. Louis and was close to his family. His father owned a small insurance agency and his mother worked as a physical therapist. He had one older brother, who was an attorney, and one older sister, who was an accountant.

When Jim came to college, he decided to major in engineering, as he had worked on a construction crew during the previous summer, and one of the engineers on the project took the time to talk with him about the profession. He admired the engineer and was impressed with what he did. He talked this over with his parents, and they seemed supportive of the idea, so he chose civil engineering as his major. His parents were proud of their children and never tried to influence their career choices in college. Unlike most of his college friends, Jim never changed his major during his undergraduate years, and he seemed reasonably satisfied with his academic studies.

When Jim graduated, his excellent academic and leadership record made him a very attractive candidate for professional positions, and after considering several offers, he accepted an engineering position with a large and prestigious corporation. The salary was excellent, the work appeared very challenging, and the opportunities for advancement were outstanding. Jim was considered by everyone to be a star with an unlimited future, and was the envy of many of his friends. His parents were also understandably proud of him.

I continued to correspond with Jim, and I was not surprised to learn that he was doing very well in his job. He was traveling around the country and after only three years, had already been promoted twice. I was pleased, yet a little puzzled that he continued to call me on the telephone, especially when he was traveling. While our conversations were friendly and focused on athletics and other college activities, I sensed that he had some other things on his mind, but was not quite ready to talk about them.

Jim continued to do very well in the corporation and joked with me that he was actually embarrassed about how much money he was being paid. After he had been with the company for about four years, Jim called me one night at home, and asked if he could come a spend a day with me on campus. Since he was several hundred miles away, I knew that he had something on his mind that was important to him, and so of course, I encouraged him to come. About 10 days later, he was in my office.

It was obvious that Jim needed to get some things off his chest, as he talked for almost an hour, telling me about his job and what he had been doing during the four years since graduation. Jim felt unfulfilled by his work, and told me he hated what he did, and could not imagine living the rest of his life working in engineering. He was pleased with his success, but his heart was not in his work at all. He talked about his high achieving older brother and sister and said he never wanted to let them or his parents down about anything. He knew they were all proud of what he had accomplished, and it was important to him that his family think highly of him. It was easy to understand that he was upset, and that I represented a non-threatening person for him to talk with about his situation. He did not want and did not expect answers from me; he just needed someone neutral that he could trust and who would listen. After having lunch with Jim and listening to him for another hour, he had to leave. He thanked me for my time, but gave no indication of what he might do in the future. Trying to humor him a bit as he left, I joked with him that I would be available for another formal confession in the future!

About a month later, Jim called and told me that he had resigned his position with the company, and had submitted an application to graduate school in his home state, with the intent of becoming a high school math teacher and coach! He had spent a long weekend with his parents, and had talked with his older brother and sister, and to his surprise, he learned that they were very supportive of his change in plans! Jim was 27 years old, but even at that age, he felt he needed the approval of his family to justify his actions! He had feared that leaving his lucrative engineering career would be a big disappointment to his family and that they would think of him as a failure. To the contrary, he found love and support from them, and he told me he felt as if he had been liberated from a burden he had been carrying around for years – yet, the only burden was one he had imagined was there.

Jim enrolled in a Master's program in math education at his state university, and completed his degree ahead of schedule. He accepted a teaching position in a comprehensive high school in a midwestern city, and also was invited to serve as assistant track coach. He loved teaching and coaching and was extremely pleased with the major change he had made in his life and career. I knew he was happy when he called me during his first semester of teaching and wanted my advice about what he should do with some bright, but unruly young students in his trigonometry class who were not working as hard as they should. "I've got to figure out a way to get these kids motivated, Doc!" he said. Then, he told me about his plans to upgrade the track program at the school, and I knew he was in the right profession! He cared about his students and he was determined to see them succeed.

Jim is now in his fifth year of teaching and coaching and is as happy as any graduate of our university I know. Whose life is it, anyway? It took him a while, but luckily, Jim decided that it was his!

My Political Naiveté

When I graduated from college in 1960, I was thrilled to become eligible to vote for the first time, having just turned 21 before the famous Nixon-Kennedy presidential election. While I was part of the so-called "silent generation" of the late 1950s, we did discuss politics quite often, and there were, of course, plenty of issues of public concern – civil rights, nuclear proliferation, the cold war, Sputnik, and the aftermath of McCarthyism. Almost all of us resented the fact that we could not vote until we were 21; after all, males had to register for the draft at age 18! Moreover, we thought we were reasonably well informed, and deserved to be full citizens at 18.

I began my student affairs career during one of most volatile and exciting decades of the last century – the '60s. Everything seemed to be changing, and the college campus was one of the primary stages where many of the social issues would be tested. When the civil rights movement captured the attention and commitment of the country, college students wanted to be part of the political process of change. As the U.S. involvement in Vietnam became more intense and controversial, students demanded a voice in decisions made by the Congress and they also wanted to be able to vote in presidential elections.

Most of my close colleagues in student affairs during the '60s were from my generation, so we were extremely pleased when the Congress passed the 26th Amendment in March, 1971, giving 18 year olds the vote! The Amendment was ratified on July 1, 1971, and this occasion was a long awaited celebration! It also seemed like a fitting and symbolic finale to the incredible social changes of the '60s decade.

I was privileged to work closely with college students during the '60s, and was enthusiastic and delighted with the passage of the 26th Amendment. I had listened to the anguish of students whose friends were sent to Vietnam, but were not old enough to vote; I had heard these students' anger at feeling disenfranchised; I had urged them to get involved in the democratic process, only to hear their frustration because they were not old enough to vote. Thus, in 1971, I was very optimistic that college students, now eligible to vote, would participate in the political process in record numbers, exercising their long awaited franchise. This newly won civic responsibility would, I believed, transform the quality and intensity of political discussion, and young people would gain an important voice in national issues. The democratic process would work!

I could not have been more wrong!

Whether in local, state, or national elections, college students in the 18-22 year old bracket not only did not vote very often; large numbers of them did not even bother to register! In almost every national election since the 26th Amendment was ratified, young people have the poorest voting record of any age category. As a result, it is relatively rare for candidates in any election to spend much time campaigning among the young, or addressing issues of primary concern to them – candidates, of course, know who votes, and are not likely to waste their time and money talking to citizens who do not vote.

Having discussed this issue for the past 30 years with colleagues, elected officials, political scientists, and young students themselves, I remain perplexed and frustrated about it. There are plenty of theories offered to explain why young college students have such a dismal voting record, but all of them sound like weak excuses to me. To my immigrant grandfather, who had only an eighth grade education, the privilege of voting was his most cherished right; he didn't learn about this in school – he had seen abuses of power in his home country, and he understood his responsibility to vote if a democracy was going to work. But, this does not help with an explanation of our current situation with college students.

Where have we missed the mark in helping young people learn this all-important democratic responsibility?

I'm still searching for the answer!

A Sweet Little Old Lady

Colleges and universities have codes of conduct, which describe the various behaviors considered to be violations of institutional standards. These codes are not municipal ordinances or state laws, but are campus regulations which students are expected to observe. They include rules about such matters as academic cheating, plagiarism, computer misuse, alcohol and drug abuse, excessive noise in residences, sexual and racial harassment, provision of false information, and disorderly behavior. There are often student-faculty judiciaries set up on the campus to assist in the handling of the various cases, and some major student organizations have procedures for monitoring the behavior of their own members. While a few students are suspended or expelled each year due to the seriousness of their offenses (mainly, academic cheating), on most campuses, the great majority of disciplinary action consists of various levels of conduct probation, and most students do not become repeat offenders. Soon after the students graduate, this part of their record is destroyed, and it is rarely reflected in the official academic transcript.

Deans of Students consider the disciplinary process to be educational in nature, even when a student must be suspended for a period of time. They are usually the "last stop" in any appeals process the student may chose to use, and they frequently become quite engaged with the student in such cases. When personal care and concern are expressed, even the most unruly and immature students often later appreciate the work of the Dean, especially when they return to school. All deans have positive stories about individual students who turned their lives around after facing the harsh realities of a campus probation or suspension, and have developed some of their closest friendships with such students. Not all cases, of course, have such happy endings, but most students who received some form of disciplinary action during their college years end up graduating. And, as alumni, most of them look back on the experience with some humor, admitting that they deserved worse than what they got!

After listening to appeals for more than 25 years, I thought I had heard every excuse imaginable from students pleading their cases. My job was to listen patiently, giving students (and their lawyers) amble opportunity to explain why the action was unwarranted or excessive, why they were actually innocent of the offense, or why the university's procedures were unfair. After listening to these appeals, I carefully weighed all the facts and reviewed the decisions of the other administrators or campus judiciaries that had made the decision. In most instances, I found that the previous decisions were justified and fair, and thus, upheld the action. In a few, where I found otherwise, I changed the sanction in some way, usually to the benefit of the student. Luckily, I always worked for presidents who did not want to be involved in these matters, and so my decisions represented the final action for students within the institution.

One day, I knew I might have a fairly lengthy appeals meeting with a student, as his file was quite thick, indicating that he had had a series of problems since he had been at the university. Moreover, he had not done well in his classes, and was only a grade or two from being dismissed for academic reasons. He had been accused of cheating on a science exam by one of his professors, and after a long hearing before a student-faculty judiciary, had been found responsible for the offense, and their decision was to suspend him from school for two full years.

When the student came in for his appeals appointment with me, his parents, his girlfriend, his brother, his grandmother, and his attorney accompanied him. I was used to meeting with students who brought their parents and others, so while I always preferred to meet just with the student, I did not object to these people being there, so long as they understood that my conversation would be primarily with the student. They were all very polite and accommodating, and we proceeded with the informal meeting.

After about an hour, during which time some of the family members became quite emotional, the student asked if we could take a break, so that he could confer with his attorney in private. I assured him that this would be okay, and after about 10 minutes, we reconvened the meeting in my office. The student, who had vigorously denied cheating on the exam during the previous hour in my office, now confessed his guilt, assuming full responsibility for his actions. Moreover, he apologized profusely for what he had done, and with tears in his eyes, extolled the virtues of the university and how much he respected it and how badly he wanted to earn his degree. He promised that he would never again engage in such activity and would be a model student who would make the university proud of him. During this emotional confession, other family members cried and provided support to the student.

The procedure I always followed in an appeal was to hear the case, and then take three or four days before I made the final decision. This was all explained in advance, of course, to the student and his family and advisers that day. After the emotions finally settled down in the office, the student and his family thanked me for considering his case and pleaded again with me to allow the student to continue in school. I had heard many students recant their earlier stories over the years, and had listened to the pleas of parents as well, so there was nothing all that unusual about this case to this point. As these several people were leaving my office, the grandmother of the student asked me if she could have a private word with me. I could not imagine what she wanted to tell me, but I was not about to refuse the polite request of a grandmother. The others left, and she and I sat down on my couch for a chat.

She appeared to be a sweet little old lady of about 80, but she took no time to get directly to the objective she had in mind. She looked me straight into the eyes, and calmly took out her purse, opened her check book, and said in a cold, matter-of-fact voice, "Ok, Dean, what will it take to get my grandson out of this mess?" I was so astonished that I froze for a moment, not knowing what to do, while not wanting to cause a ruckus in the office and escalate this situation into something ugly. Even I knew a bribe when I saw one, and without thinking, went immediately to my office door, opened it, and announced loudly to the grandmother, "why thank you, madam for coming today; I regret that I have another meeting now that I must attend." With some encouragement from me, she left the office with her fully loaded purse, and I never saw her again.

I upheld this student's two-year suspension, and he never returned to the university. Sadly, I suspect his grandmother may have taught him the same values she displayed that day in my office. So much for sweet little old ladies.

Who Has Sufficient Wisdom?

College students' lives often become complicated, and as a result, the work of student affairs staff can be challenging and ambiguous. Most student problems and issues do not lend themselves to easy answers. Fairness and equality are important concepts, but each student is unique, and flexibility is essential in the application of academic regulations and conduct rules. Faculty and staff work diligently to help students succeed and mature, but often wonder if they are making the right decisions regarding them.

Questions student affairs staff often ask are: Should a student be admitted? What can be done to help a student who is not performing well? Which student should be awarded a scholarship? How can a student with low self esteem be encouraged? How can the college help a student who constantly worries about his dysfunctional family? What conduct sanction might convince a troublesome student to change his behavior? Many faculty and staff are actively engaged with students, and to a considerable extent, measure their own effectiveness in terms of how well their students perform.

Unlike their counterparts in other countries, American colleges and universities continue to assume fairly extensive authority over the personal behavior of their students. Parents, legislators, and governing board members expect institutions to establish standards of acceptable behavior, and to take appropriate action when students do not conform to these standards. While colleges and universities no longer have a strict *in loco parentis* relationship with their students, recent legislation and court decisions confirm that institutions are expected to provide a safe campus environment, withhold financial aid from student drug abusers, and even notify parents when underage students violate alcohol laws. While the great majority of students are well behaved, the public still expects colleges and universities to have well publicized student conduct codes, and to enforce these codes in support of their educational missions.

During the past twenty years, the public's concern about sexual assault has increased greatly. Rape was once considered a crime that only strangers committed, and that rarely, if ever, occurred on college campuses. Because of the increased awareness of this crime and the willingness of citizens to discuss it more openly, education, prevention, and treatment programs have expanded dramatically. Most colleges and universities responded to this increased awareness by acknowledging that rape was a serious problem on their campuses, and by establishing counseling programs, educational activities, victim advocate services, and other support programs to address it. They also decided to add sexual assault to their student conduct codes, and by doing so, agreed to take disciplinary action against any student found guilty of rape.

When colleges and universities decided to include sexual assault in their own student conduct codes, they were both applauded and criticized. Some were pleased that institutions were finally taking action to address this serious problem; others warned that colleges were unwisely substituting themselves for the criminal courts. Rape victims obviously experience terrible trauma; they are also very reluctant (and sometimes ashamed) to report the crime to the police, or to collect sufficient evidence to make a conviction likely. Several weeks or even months may pass before a victim gathers enough courage to report the crime; after such a delay, the chance of a successful prosecution is quite low. But, apart from the criminal courts, colleges and universities can investigate an accusation brought by a rape victim, and after considering the evidence, take disciplinary action in accordance with their student conduct codes. In their zeal to demonstrate sensitivity to rape on the campus, colleges and universities have established a new, quasi-judicial system. This has made many college presidents and student affairs officers uncomfortable; on the one hand, they feel morally obligated to act against rape; on the other, they believe the college's role is not to serve as a court.

The following scenario illustrates the dilemma for colleges and universities in their sincere efforts to adjudicate rape cases on their campuses. A young woman student had been living with her student boyfriend for about five months in an apartment. They engaged in sexual intercourse fairly regularly, but one day, the woman student came to a student affairs staff member with a close friend, and reported that she had been raped two weeks earlier by her boyfriend. She had not reported this to the police, and rejected any suggestion that she do so. She did not want her parents to know anything about the incident. She said that she and her boyfriend had had a quarrel and had not seen each other for almost a week; one night, her boyfriend got drunk, and at 2:30 a.m., came to the apartment, and forced her to have sex with him. He fell asleep, and she left the apartment after the assault, and went to her friend's place. She had not been to class since the attack, and was depressed, frightened, and confused. After she was assured by the student affairs staff member that the matter would be investigated, and that it would remain completely confidential, she granted her permission for the staff member to proceed with the case.

When the young man was contacted and informed that he had been accused of rape, as described in the student conduct code, he was flabbergasted and angry. He vigorously denied the accusation, indicated that this was none of the university's business, and hired an attorney to represent him. After several weeks, the young man had a lengthy, confidential hearing conducted by a board of four faculty and two students. After listening to both the young woman and the young man (there were no witnesses), the board found the young man guilty of violating the student conduct code and the board's recommendation was to suspend him from the university for three years. He decided to appeal the case, and it was my responsibility to make the final decision for the university.

The young woman student described the incident in the same manner as she had during the hearing and to a student affairs staff member. The young man denied that he had attacked her; he said that he had begun dating another student, and by doing so, had so infuriated his current girlfriend that she made up this story to get back at him. In separate meetings with the two students, each swore they were telling the truth. Moreover, by this time, the parents of both students had become involved, and they also met with me, insisting that their children were telling the truth.

This was just one of several such sexual assault cases I had to decide. Despite the good intentions of colleges and universities to take action on such matters, I felt that, as educational institutions, this was not an appropriate role for us. But, it was my responsibility to make a final decision, and I did.

Who has sufficient wisdom to know what is right in such cases?

"Adjusted" Recommendations

Every year, dozens of students ask student affairs administrators to write letters of recommendation for them for jobs at time of graduation, for entrance into graduate and professional school programs, for sensitive government appointments, for admission to the Bar, for admission to officer training programs in the military, and for various honorary associations. Sometimes, form letters are automatically sent to student affairs offices for routine checks on disciplinary action, but in most cases, students need detailed letters, describing their character, activities, achievements, and potential. Since student affairs staff know students so well, they write lots of these letters.

There are many occasions when I have been asked to write letters of recommendation for students I have known well, and these students have been in some kind of difficulty during their undergraduate years. In most cases, they have overcome the problem, and are eligible to graduate; however, the company, agency, or professional school considering them has required them to report any problem they might have had while in college. They dutifully comply, and then I receive a formal letter of inquiry, asking me to explain the problem on behalf of the university.

Here are four examples of how I have replied:

"Dear Dr. Sandeen: James Doe has applied to our company for a position as a sales representative. Because Mr. Doe informed us that he had been placed on conduct probation during his sophomore year for an infraction of college rules, I request that you provide us with a letter explaining the details of this incident..."

I knew the student and remembered the problem. When I looked in his file, I found this police report, which stated, "James and three other students, obviously drunk, removed the large, stone sign at the chemistry building, and while attempting to place it by the music building, they dropped it, breaking off part of the sign. An officer noticed this activity, and apprehended the students, who were found sprawled on the ground next to the sign, laughing at their situation.."

The letter I wrote on behalf of James was as follows:

"James Doe has been a creative student at our college, known for his energy and his outgoing personality. He and some of his friends became a bit too boisterous one evening when he was a young sophomore and engaged in what was an unsuccessful prank. James was embarrassed by this, and made full amends for his actions. He learned from this incident, and I am confident he will do a fine job as a sales representative..."

"Dear Dr. Sandeen: We are currently considering Frank Smith for admission to the Bar. Mr. Smith indicated on his application that while an undergraduate, he was arrested on a misdemeanor charge, which was later dropped when the matter was turned over to the university for action. We would appreciate your candid description of this incident...."

I checked Mr. Smith's file and found the report, which read: "Mr. Smith was one of five students identified in a police photo taken during a streaking incident next to sorority row around midnight. When contacted, he admitted his participation and was quite embarrassed to see himself in the photo." The student had been placed on probation for a period of time.

The letter I wrote to the Bar association said, in part:

"Mr. Smith had an outstanding academic record during his undergraduate years. I am pleased he has now completed his law degree and is being considered for admission to the Bar. The minor incident in question occurred when he was very young and involved an overly demonstrative display of flirtation, which was, happily, rejected by the female students to whom it was directed. Mr. Smith matured after this isolated incident, and I know he will make a fine attorney..."

"Dear Dr. Sandeen: Jane Doe is a candidate for admission to the doctoral program in biochemistry at X University, and has listed you as a reference. Her overall academic record is excellent; however, during her sophomore year, her grades were very poor. Can you provide us with an explanation?"

I knew Jane quite well and had many discussions with her during her college years. Her parents were both successful professionals, and in 1969, Jane rebelled strongly against the Vietnam War, got involved in the psychedelic drug scene, dressed in the "hippie" clothes of the times, and vilified the "establishment" in every way she could. As a result, she almost flunked out of college and caused great strife in her family.

The letter I wrote to the biochemistry doctoral program director included this paragraph:

"Reflective of so many students during the tumultuous era when she was in college, Jane's academic progress was somewhat uneven. Perhaps her brilliance caused her to focus too narrowly at times, and other, more mundane matters were ignored. Her capacity to become fully engaged in an issue was unparalleled, but in the process, her youthful intellectual and moral passions sometimes blurred her vision. I am pleased that Jane regained her academic focus after a year of vigorously exploring alternative lifestyles...."

"Dear Dr. Sandeen: We have received an application for admission to the ABC Presbyterian Seminary from John Jones. In examining his record, we noted that Mr. Jones was suspended from your university for one year and earlier, placed on probation for two semesters. Could you kindly provide us information on this situation to help us evaluate his suitability as a future minister?"

John Jones was one of my favorite students; he was almost always in trouble, but he was so charming and persuasive that he usually avoided punishment. However, his pranks and his frequent absences from campus (he loved to hitchhike to baseball parks around the country with friends) finally got him into sufficient trouble that he was suspended for poor academic performance. He actually had been on probation twice before that, having been caught carrying out various pranks on campus (putting a goat in the Administration building; "borrowing" a portrait of the college president and placing it in a local bar; turning on the automatic sprinkling system on the soccer field during a game).

My reply to the Presbyterian seminary dean was as follows.

"As I know your seminary seeks future ministers who can relate effectively to people experiencing the full range of life's troubles, John should be considered an excellent candidate. He understands the passions and pitfalls of youth and has a wonderful sense of humor, which can be so valuable in helping others rebound from personal setbacks. He is very outgoing and his lively mind enables him to respond creatively to problems. He overcame his occasional lapses of judgment as an undergraduate, and as a result, I am confident his imagination and zest for life will make him a fine minister...."

Spring Break

Without any doubt, the greatest stress reliever ever invented for college students is Spring break! Cooped up all winter in classes and exams, students are tired, bored, and at times, depressed with the drudgery of it all. Then, the long awaited Spring break week comes, and they suddenly burst forth with renewed energy and enthusiasm. Their faces become animated, their drabby winter clothes are discarded, and their hormones erupt as they rush from the campus to any place where they can have fun. The faculty breathe a deep sigh of relief, and know when the students return after Spring break, most of their problems will somehow be diminished. It is truly a magical process and does not change from one generation to another.

For student affairs staff, Spring break week is too often synonymous with student tragedy. The exuberance of youth, especially when accompanied by too much alcohol, causes some students to lose control. Spring break week sometimes results in deaths - from falling from hotel balconies, alcohol poisoning, automobile accidents, and drowning. When a call came from the state police or relatives of a student during Spring break week, I always dreaded it, as I knew what it meant.

Of course, the great majority of students do not get themselves into trouble during Spring break week, but the image of college students drinking and partying on sunny beaches is well known throughout the country. Every year, it seemed, the national media reinforced this image of college students doing crazy things during Spring break. Just like all stereotypes, this image was wrong, and quietly, some dedicated students on many campuses decided to do something about it.

These students formed a group called "alternative spring break" and challenged their fellow students to join them for a week as volunteers in community service projects. With the help and advice of student affairs staff and faculty, they made arrangements with mental health programs, foster care facilities, retirement villages, rural school districts, substance abuse care centers, shelters for abused women, and many other programs in neighboring states. They formed teams of student volunteers who prepared themselves to be of service by living and working at these sites for a week -- at their own expense. The students asked for nothing but the opportunity to serve. Skeptics said it would never work. On my own campus, eight groups of 10-15 students turned out the first year and successfully completed their projects in five different states. The next year, the number doubled, and it continues to this day as a highly active and encouraging program, with hundreds of student participants.

The most revealing part of the "alternative spring break" program each year was a dinner the University held for the participants, during which time members of each team described their experiences. Typical of these creative students, their "descriptions" took several forms – slide and video presentations, personal testimonies, poems, written or recorded statements of gratitude from the people they served, and songs. There was, of course, lots of laughter, quite a few tears, and best of all, wide spread evidence of significant learning. The students not only learned about the endless needs of people less fortunate than themselves; they also learned how difficult and important it is to correct social injustice. But, I never saw any evidence that they would ever stop trying! All of the groups included men and women students from diverse backgrounds, and many lasting friendships were made.

This program has now become a tradition on many campuses each spring. It does not get much publicity, but it's the best Spring break week I have ever seen!

Loss of Innocence

A cold, detached examination of national statistics indicates that in a student body of 25,000 students, five or six student deaths can be expected to occur each year. But to the members of an academic community, a student death is never expected, and is not a statistic. Students are young, vibrant, and optimistic, and most of them think they will live forever! When a student dies, it is not just a sad day; it is outrageous and unfair that a bright, talented, and beautiful person should be taken from us at such a young age. For the student body, it represents the loss of innocence.

Nothing is more difficult for student affairs staff than dealing with the death of a student. Sometimes, it is their task to notify parents and family members, and of course, this can be overwhelming. They also try to provide support for the friends of the deceased student, help arrange a campus memorial service, assist family members collect personal items, and attend the funeral. Their own pain is considerable, but of course, nothing when compared to the grief felt by the family and close friends of the deceased student. It is a necessary, but arduous responsibility for student affairs staff.

Having worked in student affairs for almost four decades, I dealt with many student deaths. I can recall each one vividly, and of course, each student had his or her own special story. Despite the well-known statistics, their deaths were never expected, and being so close to the events, I could never forget them. Whether death resulted from a traffic accident, a disease, a violent act, or a suicide, the academic community reacted with grief and sorrow.

I decided to recap just one student's death out of the many that occurred during my years in student affairs, because I believe it reveals much about the lives of students.

Bob was everyone's friend. He was not a serious student, but his friends knew he was very bright, as evidenced by his quick wit and his avid reading. During his freshman year, he was placed on probation for playing various pranks on unsuspecting students in his residence hall, but he was anything but mean spirited. He had been a high school football and basketball player in his small high school, and he continued his athletic interests in college by participating in his residence hall and fraternity intramural teams. Good looking, happy-go-lucky, and gregarious, he was popular with women, and joked about dating three female students at one time. In his sophomore year, he became interested in student government, and easily won an elected seat on the student senate. He spent so much time having fun that his grades declined, and he was placed on academic probation. He promised his academic adviser (and me) that he would study harder, but he found it impossible to resist the lure of social events and time with his friends. He kept his academic problems a secret from his friends, and when his fellow senators in student government drafted him to become the senate president, he told them he could not accept because he needed to get a job and earn some money to stay in school. Of course, his grades made him ineligible to be senate president.

It was 1968, and while Bob was well informed about the Vietnam War, he was not much interested in politics, and never participated in any campus protests. He much preferred the company of his friends and fraternity brothers, partying on and off campus. He was very spontaneous and adventuresome, and one night, on a whim, he and a friend thought it would be fun to hitch-hike 350 miles to Chicago to attend a concert there, and still get back to campus in time for classes two days later. They made it, and loved recounting their trip with their friends.

After the second semester of his sophomore year, Bob returned to his hometown for the summer, where he worked in construction. He knew he had been very lax in his academic work, but he was genuinely surprised when he opened a letter from the Dean, informing him that he had been dismissed from the university for poor academic performance. He was devastated, and could not believe this had actually happened to him. He was also very embarrassed, and felt he had let his parents down. He knew he would have trouble telling his many college friends about his academic failure, even though the university informed him he could re-enroll after staying out two semesters.

Bob knew he was now likely to be drafted, since he was no longer officially enrolled at the university. So, he decided to enlist in the Army for a two-year period, telling his friends he was tired of college and that he wanted to do something different. While his friends were surprised and disappointed, they did not question Bob about his decision, knowing his adventurous spirit.

Bob was killed in Vietnam, hit by sniper fire while on a reconnaissance mission. By the time a memorial service was held on the campus several weeks later, Bob's friends knew about his earlier academic failure and his reluctance to share it with them. All of them agonized about what they might have done to prevent this terrible loss. Why had this fun loving, popular, and promising young student not felt comfortable in sharing his academic problems with his friends? This was one of the saddest days I ever experienced on any campus, and of course, there is no way to understand why such a wonderful young man had to lose his life.

Bob's college pals lost a very close friend. They also lost their innocence.

Observations and Issues

Presidents and Students

What college or university presidents do is of little concern to most undergraduates; students are focused on their academic programs, their friends, and their social activities. On most campuses, students probably know the name of their presidents, but few have actually met them, and most might not even recognize them if they saw them.

College and university presidents are pulled in many directions, and are expected to be scholars, fundraisers, lobbyists, conflict resolvers, and expert administrators. If these complex functions are not enough, they are also expected to be exemplary citizens who embody the best values of our culture: integrity, excellence, and a compassion for others. With such high expectations, it should be no surprise that so many of them fall short of these ideals.

Most college and university presidents care deeply about the education of their students and believe that as leaders, they have an obligation to speak out on public issues and take stands on important questions affecting the campus. They understand that if students are to learn about values, citizenship responsibilities, and public service, their own behavior as presidents may become very influential.

But, during the past 30 years, it was probably inevitable that a different role for college presidents would become dominant – the corporate manager. Increased pressures on academic institutions from several constituencies, especially for accountability, resulted in governing boards hiring presidents who were efficient financial managers, political experts, and fundraisers. Many of this new breed of presidents have been successful in improving the fiscal and academic performance of their institutions. But very few of them have been well known to their students, or have had much of an impact on their learning. In the process, it simply did not occur to most students that they were missing something from their presidents.

I was very fortunate to have the opportunity to work for a president for ten years who was the best leader and educator I have ever known. He was good at everything expected of him, but best of all, he earned the respect, admiration, and affection of the students. Despite his demanding schedule, he always found the time to go to student programs, banquets, residence halls, fraternity and sorority houses, student musical and dramatic activities, and athletic events. Even on a very large campus, he learned hundreds of student names, and always congratulated and thanked students for their contributions to campus life. He did not favor any one group of students, never talked about himself, and consistently focused on what students were doing. He didn't preach to students about values, but students clearly understood his passionate conviction to academic excellence, honesty, freedom of expression, and civility. He expected students to do excellent things, and they did! His presence at any student event was eagerly sought and when he spoke, he always engaged students in lively exchanges, seeking their views about how to make the university better. At every graduation exercise during his presidency, students gave him a rousing standing ovation, and he willingly posed for pictures with hundreds of them afterwards. His love for students was obvious, and it was retuned in a thousand ways.

This gifted president understood his role as a leader. He taught students about hard work, excellence, and service and re-established the president as a great teacher on the campus. His impact on the aspirations, self-esteem, and civility of students was almost beyond measure. I still correspond with many students of his era, and they always ask about him and want me to give their regards to him. All of them are extremely loyal to their university as a result of his personal leadership.

What students learn in college consists of much more than the content of their courses. They learn a great deal from adults they admire – people who respect them, appreciate their good work, and challenge them to do their very best. For a wonderful period of ten years, my faith in the values of positive leadership were restored, as I watched thousands of students benefit and learn as the result of one incredible man – their university president.

Deciding What Students Should Study

The most important and the most interesting issue in higher education is deciding what students should study. In earning their undergraduate degrees, students complete about 40 courses over a period of four years. At large universities, they select these courses from a bewildering array of up to 7000 courses. Most freshmen are uncertain and ill-informed about what their future careers might be, but often feel pressured by parents and peers to select an academic major, usually by their second year. Students have a great deal of freedom in selecting their course of study; the problem for most of them is that there are too many choices!

Most colleges and universities recognize this problem and do their best to assist students with these important academic choices. They usually require general education courses in some format, hoping to expand students' perspectives on a variety of academic subjects. Finally, they keep students' academic options open as long as possible, knowing that the majority of students will change their academic majors at least once during college.

I spent thousands of hours listening to students talk about their academic interests, their career aspirations, their courses, and their professors. They complained about classes they found boring, about professors they did not respect, and about academic regulations they viewed as unfair. They had high regard for difficult courses and for professors whose intellectual competence and dedication to teaching were outstanding. Most of all, the students questioned the relevance of courses in the humanities and social sciences which they were required to take, regardless of their academic specialization.

Typical student comments were:

"Why do I have to take this course in British History? I'm going to be an accountant, and I could be taking a management course instead?"

"This course in Art History is a waste of time for me. I'm going to medical school, and I'd rather take another science course related to my major."

"Why I have to take this French Literature class is beyond me. As a math major, I plan to work in computer science, and I see no purpose in reading French novels!"

"I'm enrolled in this Ethnic Studies course, and the reading is very time consuming and the class discussions are heated. As a chemical engineering major, I don't see the point of it all. I'd rather take another class in my major."

Convincing students of the benefits of a broad-based, liberal education is increasingly difficult, as the number of academic departments continues to grow and the world of work continues to become more specialized. Viewing this rampant specialization as inevitable, a few institutions have given in to student dissatisfaction with required courses, and have essentially abandoned their commitment to general education. My experience with students (confirmed by some actual research results!) indicates that this will prove to be a poor decision.

Almost without exception, college graduates who have been out of school for 10-15 years say that required courses in the humanities and the social sciences were among the most valuable part of their academic experience as undergraduates! Moreover, many of them chastise their alma maters for not forcing them to take more of these courses when they were in college! These same graduates are often engaged in employment not directly related to their college majors, and offer this as additional evidence that they should not have been permitted to concentrate so heavily on one academic area when they were in college. Finally, they report that the undergraduate courses that proved most relevant to their lives were these same required humanities and social science courses they disliked as students.

College and university faculty have been aware of this dilemma for many years, but understand that young students will make their own academic choices within the framework of the institution's degree requirements. Efforts to impose a standardized curriculum on undergraduates have been largely unsuccessful, and institutions eager to attract paying students are reluctant to deny students wide latitude in course selection.

I loved listening to students' comments about their course work, their professors, and their academic requirements. When they asked, I shared my views about their academic programs. I saw no evidence that any students ever changed their minds as a result, but I certainly enjoyed hearing their comments 15 years later!

Student Satisfaction and Retention

The "enrollment management" function in college and universities is critical to the success and survival of many institutions. Admissions personnel publish attractive brochures describing their campuses, develop dazzling web sites about their institutions, visit high schools throughout the year, conduct daily tours of their campuses, seek scholarship money to attract students, and talk directly with prospective students and their parents. Moreover, they work hard to improve their "yield" each year regarding the students they admit; that is, the percentage of students who accept the invitation for admission and actually enroll. Even at some selective colleges and universities, if 45 students enroll out of 100 admitted, this is considered a good yield. When the yield decreases, and the number of new freshmen does not meet the institution's goal, it is often the Director of Admissions who is blamed. The pressure on admissions officers to deliver a freshman class of the right number, no less the right combination of gender, race, geography, and academic ability is very high.

The competition for students with outstanding academic, artistic, musical, and athletic abilities is quite stiff, and colleges and universities also recruit students from a variety of ethnic and racial backgrounds to ensure diversity. This requires a good deal of coordination between admissions and financial aid staff, as many outstanding students decide to enroll at a college based upon the financial "package" the institution offers to them. This scramble for students with special talents has caused many colleges and universities to seek more scholarship gifts in their fund raising programs, as the competition to attract these students has become so stiff.

The retention of enrolled students is another important aspect of enrollment management. A few colleges and universities are fortunate to graduate 90 percent of their students over a four-year period; for the majority of other institutions, the figure is under 50 percent. Obviously, a college wants to retain its students once they are enrolled. But, students leave college for a great variety of reasons, and often, these reasons are personal rather than academic in nature. Most institutions study this matter quite closely by asking students who leave before graduation why they are withdrawing. While such efforts can be quite instructive, the answers students give quite often mask the real reasons they decide to leave. For a college whose budget is very dependent on student tuition, a serious retention problem can mean financial disaster. This is serious business for many colleges and universities, and as a result, a lively private industry has developed around this issue during the past 20 years. For a fee, consultants will visit a campus, study the retention problem in detail, and help the college develop new plans and strategies that will hopefully correct the problem.

There has been a good deal of research done on college student retention, and much of it has been quite helpful to colleges and universities in addressing this issue. As a result, comprehensive programs have been suggested to institutions to improve their retention. These programs might include advertising, new publications, new curricula, upgraded residence halls, new sports and recreation facilities, closer faculty-student relations, study abroad opportunities, independent study, improved personal advising, and other activities thought to be helpful. Some of these efforts have, indeed, resulted in increased student satisfaction and retention at some institutions. While I am encouraged with the research on retention, my years of experience of working directly with students indicates that there are often very personal and complicated reasons why students like or dislike their institutions, and thus, decide to stay or leave. Here are a few examples.

A young freshman was very unhappy at our university during his first semester. His residence hall adviser said he stayed in his room, did not socialize much, and did not attend campus concerts or athletic events. His first semester grades were adequate, but a good deal lower than one would expect from his College Board scores. After hearing from his parents, who were quite distraught over his unhappiness in college, I contacted the student, and he came to my office for a visit. He was very polite, but he said he didn't like his classes, the faculty were lousy teachers, the food in the dining halls was terrible, and the campus itself was not very attractive. He said he anticipated that he would be transferring to another institution after his second semester. He didn't follow up on any of the suggestions I made to him, and I thought this student would surely leave. Almost three months later, right before the end of the semester, I saw the student on campus and to my surprise, he told me with great enthusiasm about his academic plans for the coming fall at our university. After some conversation, I asked him if he felt the same way about the institution as he had before. The student laughed, and said, "Oh, no! I love this place – it's great." What had happened that so dramatically changed his view of the institution? He fell in love with a young woman he met in one of his classes! By his senior year, he was serving as a volunteer tour guide for the admissions office, wearing the school colors, and singing the praises of his university to prospective students!

I met another student one day who was in the process of leaving the institution. He wrote on his withdrawal form, "personal" as the reason for leaving. While we respect the privacy of students, and do not push them to reveal anything they prefer to keep to themselves, I was able to begin a conversation with this student and what I learned made me determined to help him. After he became comfortable with me, the student told me that he had been working 35 hours per week, while taking a full academic load of courses, in order to earn money to send home to his mother. She was unable to work, and this student felt guilty about being in college while his mother could barely make ends meet at home. Thus, he thought his only option was to leave college, return home, and get a full time job to support his mother. Thanks to some excellent work by our financial aid staff, we were able to help this student, and make it possible for him to remain in school. He loved the university and for years now, has been a grateful graduate. It is unlikely that any "enrollment management" gimmick or research study would have identified this student's problem.

I worked at one university where many of the undergraduates did not have frequent out of class contacts with their faculty. Most students did not complain about this, as they probably did not expect anything different. Faculty held their required office hours each week, and talked with students who came by at such times, but not many students took advantage of this opportunity. While this institution was very popular and most students liked being there, some academic departments expressed concern about not attracting as many majors as they had in past years, and others complained that too many of their majors left their department after only a year, deciding to select another academic field. In reviewing this matter, I examined the statistics for the 85 academic departments on the campus, and discovered one whose record was stunning: it had more students each year, and it retained and graduated almost all of them! What was it about this department that made it unique? I found out with very little effort. A visit to the department revealed a friendly, student centered atmosphere, where faculty called students by their names. There were pictures of student-faculty social and athletic events on the walls, and awards recognizing outstanding student achievements as well. Most important, I learned that a faculty member actually visited with a student and his or her parents, in the student's home, as part of the faculty's advising responsibilities. Students worked hard in this department, but felt appreciated. No wonder they had the highest graduation rate of any department on the campus!

I knew another student who was a very gifted mathematician and was doing excellent work at the university. I actually met him on the squash courts, where he and I enjoyed a game a couple of times per month. He had a difficult conflict with his parents, who were divorced. His father had required this young man to attend our university, despite the boy's intent to go to a smaller, out-of-state college, where he could pursue his real dream - playing intercollegiate soccer. The father would not permit the young man to transfer, despite his fine academic record. In talking with this student several times, I was pleased to learn that his mother eventually intervened, and offered to pay her son's tuition at the out of state college. The student left our university, transferred to the small college, and earned two letters as a member of the soccer team. This student would most likely appear in some statistical study as part of a "retention failure." I prefer to think of him as a real success!

Recruiting New Students

In the mid-1960s, the civil rights movement had a profound influence on American society, and most traditionally white colleges and universities responded by recruiting more African-American students. While these efforts were almost always well intentioned, they were often characterized by poor planning, inadequate funding, and insufficient support services for the students. Many of these new students were under prepared academically, and their subsequent poor classroom performance often resulted in failure. Others worked hard, but found the culture of the campus so unwelcoming that they dropped out and returned home. Many succeeded, despite the odds and the often tense racial climate at the institution.

Most colleges and universities did not knowingly discriminate in their admissions policies, but of course, only a tiny fraction of the student bodies of the best known public and private universities during their time consisted of African-American students. Reflecting the national commitment of the times to social justice and equal opportunity, colleges and universities embraced the concept of affirmative action in the hiring of faculty and staff, and in the recruitment of students in increase the diversity of their institutions. This was a volatile, yet exciting time in higher education, as change was taking place rapidly, and the climate was very receptive to new ideas and programs.

In 1968, a student affairs colleague and I requested permission of our president to invite African-American students to an open meeting so that we might gain a better understanding of their experiences, needs, and aspirations. There was some reluctance to do this, as some white leaders still believed it was better "not to stir things up too much!" Luckily, this president was an exception, and we issue the invitation. There were only about 200 African-American students at this institution of over 19,000, which was located in a small town in a Midwestern state with a very small minority population. About 80 students attended the meeting and expressed genuine surprise and appreciation – they said that no one had paid them any special attention before! They were, however, wary of what these young, white administrators might want from them, despite the fact that my colleague and I knew many of the students fairly well.

The conversation was open, revealing, and sometimes, hostile and funny. The students talked about feeling isolated and lonely and said that they did not relate at all to the traditions of the institution. They had respect for their faculty, but emphasized that "all they wanted from this place was a degree," so that they could get a good job after graduation. Almost to a person, they said if they had it to do over again, they would not have attended the institution, as they did not feel welcome here and they felt that the white students misunderstood them and looked down upon them socially. These statements from the students were painful for us to hear, but they reflected accurately what African-American students were saying on many other white campuses during this decade. We accepted them as true, and assured the students we would like to work with them to improve their lives at the university. They were skeptical of anything we could do, but politely thanked us for our willingness to listen to them.

After the meeting was over, a group of about ten women students asked to talk with my colleague and me about a specific issue. We sat down with them and they quickly came to the point they wanted to make: "Please recruit some more African-American men – we are lonesome!" They were right, of course; only one out of three African-American students was male, and this limited their social life on campus. We asked them if they would be willing to help in the recruitment of African-American students. Despite their negative descriptions of their experiences at the university, they quickly volunteered to help and expressed enthusiasm with this prospect.

With the help of many people in the next few weeks, my colleague and I secured the permission (and the financial support!) of the university's president to travel to a large city where arrangements had been made for us to visit with some prospective African-American students. So, we drove several hours to the city, and after two or three more visits and many phone calls and letters, we were able to recruit and enroll 25 new African-American students when classes began in the fall. We had no grand plan, but we did have the good will and support of many students, faculty, staff, and community members. Whether we encountered problems in housing, financial aid, health, academic advising, conduct, or poor grades, there were people willing to help.

Not all of this original group of 25 graduated, of course. Some of them simply did not like the university or its rural location, and some did not succeed academically. But, most of them did succeed, and their presence led to increased efforts by the institution to hire more African-American faculty and staff, and especially, to recruit more African-American students. Only ten years after this program was initiated, the university's enrollment of African-American students had more than tripled.

My colleague and I remained closely engaged with the original group of recruited students, and fortunately, a newly created office was soon established that assumed responsibility for the recruitment and support of African-American students. We became well acquainted with the first group of 25 students and became quite attached to them. Very late one evening, one of the students (a junior by this time) got into an argument at a local bar, and had his eye injured in a fight. When he had to be taken to an emergency room at the local hospital for medical attention, I was called at home and went immediately to the hospital. The student, who had had too much to drink, was not very cooperative with the medical staff, but eventually settled down. One of the doctors, knowing that I was the representative of the university, angrily lectured me that "such students have no place at the university!" He went on to tell me that he had three university degrees and he could tell when a student was academically qualified. It was at this point that I lost my temper and told him to mind his medical business and I would tend to the university's business! We almost came to blows ourselves that night in the emergency room, but luckily, we avoided it. After the student got a few stitches over his eye, I took him home. A couple of years later, he graduated, and after returning for a Master's degree, he now enjoys a successful career as a school administrator.

My colleague and I received some criticism, much of it justified, for the way we conducted this recruitment and support program. We were not as well organized as we should have been, and we often allowed our own personal feelings to influence what was done to assist these students. There were some students who did not succeed, but the students who did succeed made the effort worthwhile. One of the students worked for the university in admissions and financial aid herself for many years after earning her degree. My colleague and I had great fun teasing her about her enthusiastic and positive descriptions of the institution to the prospective students she herself was now recruiting!

Reference Points

For each generation of students, there is some signal event, some yardstick, which becomes a common reference point for them. Many students seem to measure their lives from that event forward, and many of them are profoundly affected by the event. For earlier generations, it might have been Armistice Day, the stock market crash, Pearl Harbor, the death of FDR, the bombing of Hiroshima and Nagasaki, or the launching of Sputnik. People who were in college when those events occurred can remember where they were and what they were doing at the time, even 50 years later. The shock of these dramatic events affects all people, of course, but the impact on young, idealistic college students can be profound.

I was a live-in director of a residence hall of 1200 students in 1963 when, about noon on Friday, November 22 the news of President John F.Kennedy's assassination was announced. Almost at once, a terrible silence came over the hall, the large dining room, and meeting areas. This was before the days when students had television sets in their rooms, so we quickly set up televisions in several large rooms, and for the next four days, hundreds of shocked students sat mesmerized, watching the incredible events unfold. My wife and I opened our apartment to students, and they filled every available space in it; they were numbed by this event, but they wanted to be with others they knew. John Kennedy was the idol of this generation, and his assassination represented a terrible loss of innocence for them. The resulting absence of inspired leadership in ensuing years certainly contributed greatly to the disillusionment with government later in the '60s. I have remained in contact with some of these students, and now, 38 years later, every one of them talks about that event as a turning point in their lives and as a defining moment for them.

A few years later, I was having dinner at a restaurant with a job candidate when I received a phone call from a colleague, informing me that Martin Luther King, Jr. had been assassinated in Memphis. It was about 9:00 p.m. on Thursday, April 4, 1968. I immediately left the restaurant and went to campus, where we quickly worked to arrange some meetings with students. The elected leaders of the major student organizations met with us and campus ministers late into the night, planning how we might respond to this tragedy. Turmoil in the country was great, with the Vietnam War escalating and the civil rights movement exploding into riots in Detroit the previous year. We had worked very hard to recruit additional African-American students to the University this year, and now, everything seemed to be coming apart. The rest of that spring semester, there was a lot of anger and frustration, as students struggled to comprehend what was happening in their lives. Many of these students were too young to have been greatly affected by the JFK assassination; it was the MLK tragedy that was the defining public event in their lives. When Robert Kennedy was killed two months later and then, the riots took place at the Democratic national convention in Chicago, 1968 became not just a date for these students; it became a benchmark from which they would forever mark their lives.

The undergraduate student cohort turns over rapidly, of course, and even though it was only two years later, the tragic shootings at Kent State University on Monday, May 4, 1970 marked yet another signal event in the lives of college students. I was a dean of students at the time, and the country was teeming with protests in reaction to President Nixon's decision two days earlier to move the war into Cambodia. When the news of the Kent State deaths became known, there was the strongest and most emotional reaction by students I have seen. There was incredible anger, and the outraged young people did not know what to do; on our campus, they almost instinctively went to the most visible intersection and simply sat down. There was no violence, and the police effectively rerouted traffic. Six or seven thousand students simply sat down in a massive, peaceful protest. Microphones were brought in and speeches were made, but mainly, students just wanted to be together, and this continued for almost three days. I had never witnessed a time when so many outstanding young people had lost complete confidence in and respect for their government. Watergate was to follow the next year, of course, but it was the Kent State tragedy that served as the yardstick for these students, causing them to become very cynical about their country and its future. Young college students at this time remember Kent State as an end and a beginning in their lives.

The next defining moment for young college students occurred on January 28, 1986, when the space shuttle *Challenger* exploded, killing all seven aboard, including Krista McCauliff, a teacher. This event did not result in any public protests or campus demonstrations; it was so shocking to see the explosion as it happened, on television, that it had an enormous impact on young people. They identified with the charismatic young teacher, and when her life ended right before their eyes, it was a terrible loss of innocence. It was as if they had lost a close friend; this was a personal event - not a political one. Students who were in college in 1986 can recall where they were on that day, and these students have marked this event as a significant benchmark in their lives.

Perhaps reflective of the affluent, non-political nature of the '90s decade, students enrolled during this time clearly identify the O.J. Simpson trial of 1995 as their defining public event. The trial probably stimulated more debate and conversation between whites and African-American students that any other event. It was dominant for so long on the national news that it became part of daily discussion on the campus for months. It is not clear what impact the trial had on college students; but there is no doubt that students at that time use the Simpson trial as a point of reference in their lives. It was the "main event" for their generation!

I have attended dozens of alumni meetings and class reunions for many years, and the conversation at these events always turns to these "points of reference" that occurred during their college years. For better or for worse, these events helped to define who they were and served as benchmarks in their lives.

Insight and Inspiration

He's My Brother

Gay, lesbian, and bi-sexual students have faced some of the most blatant discrimination in colleges and universities. Prior to about 1970, these students led much of their lives in secret, keeping the truth of their sexuality from friends, potential employers, and family members. They were painfully aware of the homophobic attitudes that were often publicly expressed on the campus, and of the derisive "humor" directed at homosexuals. While colleges vigorously proclaimed their commitment to diversity, gay, lesbian, and bisexual students were not included in this effort. Most of the academic community pretended that there was no problem; worse, the majority acted as if these students were not there.

Of course, there were gay, lesbian, and bi-sexual faculty and staff on the campus as well, and they faced similar, and perhaps even more ominous obstacles. However competent they might be as professionals, they understood that if their sexuality were revealed, their jobs and advancement opportunities might be in jeopardy. Moreover, many of them had to restrict their social lives, avoiding places where they might be seen with their partner, and making up stories to explain their absence at various events. Many of them tried to reach out to gay, lesbian, and bi-sexual students to help these young people with their personal struggles, but the faculty and staff who did so knew they might risk their own jobs in the process.

Some student affairs staff were viewed with sufficient trust that gay, lesbian, and bi-sexual students might talk honestly with them about their lives and experiences at the university. But even this process had to be conducted without any publicity or invitation; gay, lesbian, and bi-sexual students quietly passed word among themselves information about which staff could be trusted and were willing to be helpful. Many student affairs staff, of course, felt hypocritical about this process, choosing public silence on the issue to preserve their positions.

Probably due to a complex set of factors, public attitudes toward gay, lesbian, and bi-sexual citizens began to change during the late 1970s. When the AIDS virus was discovered in the early 1980s, and several well-known public figures revealed they were gay, there seemed to be growing tolerance and understanding. The issue became more openly discussed; gay-rights organizations grew rapidly; popular television programs included gay characters; and efforts were made to include sexual orientation in existing anti-discrimination laws. Gay, lesbian, and bi-sexual student organizations were established on most campuses, and for the first time, many students openly and proudly declared their sexual orientation on designated "coming out days." Some gay faculty and staff found increased understanding and acceptance among their colleagues, and did the same.

But many of the old, homophobic attitudes persisted on campuses, and gay, lesbian, and bi-sexual students continued to struggle for acceptance. When a University of Wyoming gay student was tortured and murdered after being abducted from a bar in 1999, the nation was dramatically reminded of the terrible ramifications of hate. It was viewed, accurately, as the current day version of lynching. Despite significant advances in education and awareness, gay, lesbian, and bi-sexual students continued to face rejection and hostility on their campuses.

I knew an outstanding male student leader on our campus, and after working with him in a variety of campus activities for about two years, he told me one day in my office that he was gay. He said he had not shared this information with anyone else on campus and that for the last few years, his life had been a nightmare. He was convinced that if his family knew about his sexual orientation, they would immediately reject him. He loved his involvement in campus life and was a very successful leader, having been elected to offices in the student union and in his fraternity. He was well aware of the snide remarks and off-color jokes about homosexuals throughout the campus, and felt that he would "lose everything" if his friends knew he was gay. He was especially worried about the members of his fraternity; he joked that if there was any organization that has a reputation for homophobia, it is a college fraternity! After more conversations during the next few months, this student accepted my suggestion that he talk with one of our staff, who was especially effective in helping gay students.

In the first semester of his senior year, this student quietly participated in the campus "coming out" day, declaring openly his sexual orientation. At his request, I was among the small crowd that gathered for this occasion. It was a very emotional time for this student, and of course, a very important step in his personal development. In one of the most heartwarming and encouraging demonstrations of friendship and support I have seen, this young man that day was accompanied by many of his fraternity brothers and his fellow officers on the student union board. By their presence, they wanted him and others to know that he was their friend.

Since the gay student was a well known campus leader, a reporter from the student newspaper was there, and asked one of the gay student's fraternity brothers why he was present for this event. His simple response was, "He's my brother."

To me, that is the essence of what we are trying to teach.

It's No Big Deal

Most colleges and universities paid little attention to students with disabilities until the civil rights movement helped to raise awareness of discrimination against various groups in American society. This eventually resulted in significant federal legislation in 1973 and then, the Americans with Disabilities Act, passed by Congress in 1991. The doors of higher education finally were opened to those with disabilities, and colleges and universities were legally obligated to admit academically qualified students without regard to disability, and to make reasonable accommodations for them in their academic programs, and in student life.

As a result of increased public awareness, changed attitudes of college administrators and faculty, and the new laws, enrollment of students with disabilities has increased dramatically during the past twenty years. Colleges have adapted their physical facilities, their academic policies, and their own attitudes in efforts to help these students succeed. In the 1970s and early 1980s, institutions concentrated mainly on making their classrooms, laboratories, residence halls, walkways, and other facilities accessible to persons with physical disabilities. Since that time, large numbers of students with learning disabilities have enrolled, and many institutions are finding that the academic accommodations required for these students are very challenging.

Since students are not required to inform a college about their disability during the application process, it is somewhat difficult for colleges to predict the number of students with disabilities who will enroll each year. However, given the relatively brief number of years that significant numbers of students with disabilities have come to college, the overall record is quite encouraging regarding their graduation rates and success after college.

On most campuses, the student affairs staff assumes the primary responsibility for assisting students with disabilities, and there is usually a special office staffed with professionals whose role it is to work with them. These staff serve as advocates, help orient the new students to the campus, arrange for necessary testing, find note takers, assist with living arrangements, work with faculty, and provide whatever support is necessary for the students' success. They also frequently serve as counselors and advisers to many of the students, respond to inquiries from the students' families, and encourage the students to get involved in various campus activities and programs.

During one year on our campus, a group of students with physical disabilities formed their own student organization, calling it PLUS, an acronym for Physically Limited University Students. Mary, their adviser, was an amazing young student affairs staff member who was successful in encouraging their involvement in campus politics, student government, and various social activities. With her help, the PLUS group conducted its own leadership retreat one weekend at a camp thirty miles from campus, and all of us who attended learned a great deal. Mary took seriously her belief that students with disabilities could do just about anything on campus, and she and the students had a lot of fun doing just that!

Mary startled the rest of the student affairs staff one day when she casually informed us that she and the students with disabilities group were going on a camping and canoeing weekend trip! We knew she was determined to demonstrate to the students themselves that they could do just about anything, but we wondered how she could do this. Moreover, as the senior administrator, I had to worry about liability as well. "What if one of the students were to fall out of the canoe," I asked? Mary just laughed, and answered, "Well, of course, someone will fall out of a canoe – that's why we've been training for the past two weeks with our life jackets. It's been a real hoot!"

Mary and about 15 students went on the weekend camping and canoeing trip, and by all accounts, everyone had a wonderful time. Several of us listened to a recounting of the trip a week later at the group's regular meeting, and we all enjoyed a lot of laughter with the students. I pretended not to listen when the students joked about the two cases of beer they had hidden in one of the canoes! No doubt this contributed to their good times! Most important, it was thrilling to see what one dedicated adviser could do to build confidence, encourage friendships, and involve students in the life of the university.

Later, we all thanked Mary and asked her how in the world she managed to do this. Always modest, this amazing young adviser replied with her usual grin, "Hey – it's no big deal!"

This is what I call great teaching in student affairs!

The Faculty Just Don't Care

The American public often misunderstands college and university professors. The old image of "Mr. Chips" is gone, but humorous stories about the absent minded professor are still quite common. College faculty are respected for their knowledge and they are often asked to comment publicly on issues related to their specialties. But, many members of the public have disdain for the concept of faculty tenure, and are resentful for what they perceive to be a privileged status held by professors. There are also feelings among some citizens that faculty have too much free time, that they do not teach enough, that they ignore the personal needs of their students, and that they spend too much time on research.

It is not unusual for college and university administrators to become quite isolated on their own campuses. Many of them work long hours, and have little contact with students or faculty. As a result, some administrators feel almost separate from their own institutions, and may view their job at the college in the same way they might if they worked for a private company. It was irritating to me during my career to listen to the uninformed complaints of some administrative staff as they referred to faculty as lazy, radical, or selfish. I regret to say that some student affairs staff expressed similar views, perhaps revealing a lack of confidence in their own work, or a feeling of envy for the faculty.

Since I taught classes every year as an administrator, some of my colleagues asked me why I did not assume a full time faculty role. Their admonition was based upon their view that life as a faculty member would be much easier than serving as an administrator and that anyone who had such an option ought to take it! This gap in understanding between faculty and administrators is well known, of course, and often goes both ways, with some faculty stereotyping administrators as paper shuffling bureaucrats, disconnected from any useful academic function.

One of the realities of working in student affairs is knowing that there will never be enough staff to meet all of the needs of the students. Moreover, no student affairs staff has sufficient knowledge or expertise to address effectively all of the problems and issues needing attention, nor the financial resources adequate to do so. But, student affairs staff have the most marvelous resource available to anyone - the faculty on its own campus! I was very fortunate to be able to develop positive relationships with many faculty, and our student affairs division was highly dependent upon them for their advice, expertise, and participation in a wide variety of extra-curricular programs. I lost patience with those who complained about faculty being so focused on their own work that they would not contribute their time and talents to other areas of the campus; my experience with faculty was just the opposite. To those who whined, "The faculty just don't care," I offer the following as examples of the many who did:

In the 1970s, when we were looking for new approaches to dealing with student alcohol abuse, we began a series of conversations with faculty in medicine, law, sociology, and pharmacy, seeking their advice about how to develop educationally based programs. The result was a collaborative grant proposal, enabling us to build an alcohol education model that was eventually replicated on many other campuses. It would never have happened if several faculty members had not volunteered their time, expertise, and support. And, all we had to do was ask.

During the Vietnam War years, a group of about 200 students broke into the Army R.O.T.C. building one night and vowed to stay there until the University would agree to drop all of its research projects with the Department of Defense. Several of us in student affairs had established informal relationships with faculty who were visible and respected by students. We knew we could count on these faculty to help in any crisis of this kind. When we got to the armory, we called these faculty, and over 50 of them came immediately to the facility. The student protestors had expected a confrontation with the police; instead, we invited faculty to come and talk with the students, which they did until after 3:00 a.m Without threatening any students, the occupation of the building ended peacefully before classes resumed the next morning, and everyone left. By their genuine concern, their willingness to listen, and their physical presence, the faculty averted a potentially explosive problem.

Dozens of faculty members volunteer their time as advisers to student organizations. They contribute to the success of these organizations and most important, to the education and growth of the student members. At one university where I worked, a faculty member was asked to serve as the adviser to a special council of students which was responsible for inviting distinguished speakers to the campus. He never interfered with the students' decisions, but he was so highly respected by the students that they always sought his advice. This highly visible program made the students responsible for it very vulnerable to criticism by those who thought the invited speakers should not be so controversial. The faculty member and his wife invited each distinguished speaker and the 12 students involved in the program to an elegant dinner at their home, and this occurred 7 or 8 times per year for 13 years, when the faculty member retired. Moreover, the faculty member and his wife prepared and paid for these dinners themselves. In the process, the students who attended them had their lives enriched and their educations enhanced.

A terrible tragedy occurred one day on our campus when a Japanese graduate student took his own life. Perplexed about how best to contact his family members in Japan, we immediately turned to a faculty member we knew who spoke Japanese. She not only counseled us on how to proceed, but also volunteered herself to break this terrible news to the family. She understood the culture, had traveled extensively in Japan, and knew how to deal with officials there. After her many conversations with the family, she eventually arranged to meet with them in their home city, and traveled to Japan with the student's remains. In an extremely difficult situation, this faculty member personalized the university in the best possible way.

During a time of serious racial turmoil on the campus, some of us in student affairs thought an off campus weekend retreat with white and black student leaders might improve understanding among these students. We knew it was important to get faculty members there for the weekend and so we asked 20 professors if they would be willing to participate. Almost all of them attended, and most of them stayed up late at night, talking informally with the students. Just by being there and showing they cared about the students helped to ease tensions on the campus. Many of these faculty later served as informal advisers and mentors to some of the students they met during that weekend retreat.

A mathematics professor noted that one of her students was doing poorly in her calculus class. The professor called the student in and arranged tutoring sessions for the student, but later discovered that the student was very upset over her parent's impending divorce, and was thinking about quitting school. The faculty member and her husband invited the student to their home for dinner, and over the next two years, served as surrogate parents for her. The student earned her degree, and says she owes her success to this faculty member and her husband.

Those who think faculty do not care about their students just do not know any faculty members very well!

A Lesson From a Student

Freedom of expression is the most cherished value in American colleges and universities. If new insights are to be achieved, faculty must be free to pursue their subjects without regard to political, religious, or economic influence or pressure. In teaching and in research, this freedom is essential to academic excellence.

Students must be free, as well to read, to study, and to pursue academic, social, and political issues if they are to learn effectively. Students learn to accept responsibility by having it, and they learn about the truth in an atmosphere of free inquiry, debate, and discussion. These principles are so well established in American higher education that they are often taken for granted. But, it took almost two centuries in this country before faculty at most colleges were granted real academic freedom, and even longer for students to be considered mature enough to make their own academic decisions.

A college's commitment to freedom of expression is often revealed in its policy regarding the invitation of external speakers to the campus for various forums, seminars, and lectures. In particular, this can be very instructive as it relates to student organizations, which frequently are the sponsoring groups for invited speakers. As recently as 1960, some public colleges and universities did not permit student organizations to invite controversial (for example, communist) speakers to their campuses. The public rationale was that such speakers might easily sway young undergraduates, and the college should protect them from dangerous ideas; the more likely reason was that legislators and other public officials might withdraw financial support from the college if such unpopular speakers were allowed to come to the campus. Student leaders, of course, were well aware of such hypocrisy, and delighted in tormenting college administrators by attempting to invite the most controversial speakers they could find.

When the campuses became a prime stage for the discussion of the most volatile public issues during the civil rights movement and the Vietnam War, freedom of expression was subjected to rigorous tests. Despite a great deal of noise and turmoil, this cherished constitutional and academic value survived, and indeed, became stronger. Prior restraints placed upon student organizations regarding invited speakers were eliminated at most public institutions. College presidents and others argued that if students were to make informed and enlightened decisions on important issues, they must be free to examine all ideas and points of view. This not only improved the quality of education for students; it also enlivened and upgraded the nature of student life itself.

Many religious, political, and economic student groups invite speakers to their campuses during the year, as part of their purpose as groups is to enhance or influence the quality of discourse on topics of concern to them. On large campuses, where there are hundreds of student organizations, it is difficult to gain the attention of large segments of the student body on any single issue, as there is so much competition. In any given week, there may be twenty or thirty speakers appearing on the campus in various locations. This lively activity is considered routine and it affirms the value of the free and open marketplace of ideas in American higher education.

Despite the freedom now enjoyed by student groups to invite speakers of their own choosing, occasionally a student group brings to the campus someone whose mere presence evokes strong reactions and protests from others, both in and outside of the academic community. This happened a few years ago when an African-American student group (there were over 20 campus groups with the prefix "African-American, depending on their interests!) invited a well-known leader from the Nation of Islam to the campus. Many students and faculty, upon learning of the invitation, voiced their objections, based upon printed reports from other campuses that indicated this speaker had made anti-Semitic and anti-Christian remarks. Moreover, the objectors argued that this speaker had no respectable academic credentials, and in previous presentations, had used vicious "street rhetoric" in denouncing public officials, sometimes resulting in fights among the audience. The student group who invited this speaker, originally expecting perhaps 50 people for the event, now had created a campus issue, and if the event could be held safely, it would have to be moved to an auditorium where more than 800 might attend.

The student affairs staff is usually expected to make sure such potentially volatile events take place with a minimum amount of trouble. Because of the angry tone of the campus conversations about this event during the week preceding it, we invited leaders of the sponsoring student organization to meet with faculty and students who had been objecting vigorously to the choice of the speaker. The rhetoric at the three meetings we convened for this purpose that week was often rancorous; feelings between African-American students and faculty and Jewish students and faculty were especially tense. There were frequent accusations and very little mutual understanding. We understood that if this speech was going to take place, it would require a good deal of supervision on our part, as some hecklers were determined to prevent the Nation of Islam representative from speaking at all.

But, during the third meeting among the sponsoring student group and their critics, a very positive development occurred. A Jewish faculty member, who was highly respected by the students on both sides of the issue, asked the student president of the African-American sponsoring group, "Why would you invite a person whose ideas are so reprehensible and so insulting to some people on our campus?" The young woman leader calmly responded to the professor with a question of her own: "Why would you assume that just because our organization invited the speaker that we might agree with him?" She went on to say that her organization had invited speakers during the year to the campus that represented quite different points of view, and that this, after all, is the purpose of a free exchange of ideas. The faculty member not only acknowledged her insight; he thanked her for expressing it so well, and this enabled those present at the meeting to work together more constructively.

The speech was made to a packed auditorium, and it was frequently interrupted by shouted objections. A few unruly persons in the audience had to be removed, but the speech was completed without any serious incidents. Weeks later, few people in attendance probably remembered much of the substance of the speech. However, everyone on the campus developed a greater understanding of the importance of freedom of expression and the value of allowing students to be exposed to ideas, even when these ideas may be repugnant to others.

Most important to me was the personal exchange that took place between the Jewish faculty member and the African-American student. A wise and thoughtful faculty member recognized that a young student had taught him and others present at the meeting a valuable lesson about freedom of expression.

Whose Flag Is That, Anyway?

For many decades, the Reserve Officer Training Corps (ROTC) programs were highly respected and admired on American campuses, as they prepared talented and dedicated young men and women for leadership in the United States Army, Navy, Air Force, and Marines. The original "land-grant" act, passed by Congress in 1862, included a provision that these colleges would have military training as part of their curricula. Some of the brightest students were engaged in the ROTC programs and the drills and ceremonies conducted on the campuses were a well-accepted part of college life. Formal military reviews each year attracted crowds of faculty, students, parents, and community members. Students who were commissioned as officers at graduation were given special recognition and were often among the top scholars and leaders in their class.

When the United States became involved in the Vietnam conflict, graduates of ROTC programs were prominent leaders in the military effort. By 1967, when a good deal of public opinion had shifted against U.S. involvement in the war, the ROTC programs on the campuses became the most visible target for student protesters. Opponents of the war, who demanded that ROTC be banned from the campuses, vilified the programs and the students enrolled in them. At many colleges and universities, this controversy erupted into ugly confrontations and violence. Disruption of military drills was a common tactic, and in a few instances, armories on campus were set afire by protesters.

Luckily for the campuses, most of the protesters did not physically attack the students who were enrolled in the ROTC programs themselves. Their anger was mainly directed at the presence of the ROTC programs as part of the universities, and to the college presidents who were responsible for them. Given the frequent and poisonous rhetoric, it is remarkable that the students enrolled in the ROTC programs did not retaliate against their tormentors. The excellent training and supervision they received from their professors of military science, no doubt, made the difference.

After the U.S. bombing of Haiphong Harbor in 1972, another series of mass protests occurred around the country, and particularly, on college campuses. At our university, the object of the protesters became the Navy ROTC building, located in the central part of the campus. The crowd probably numbered about 1500, which was a small percentage of the student body, but nevertheless, sufficient to cause a potentially serious problem.. Thanks to the enlightened and thoughtful leadership of the University's president, we had managed to handle our own affairs without the intervention of state police or the National Guard. Despite criticism from some elected officials and alumni, who thought we should "get tough" and expel protesting students from the university, the President knew the best way to handle large protests was to work closely with the students, show patience and understanding, and allow matters to calm down after a few days. Since the protests against the war had begun on the campus in 1965, his strategy had proved highly successful.

At about 1:00 in the afternoon, the crowd surrounded the Navy ROTC building and began shouting, "no more war," and "ROTC off campus." With the large, excitable crowd making a lot of noise, no one noticed that a couple of students had managed to climb onto the roof of the building, and had removed the U.S. flag and replaced it with the North Vietnamese flag! A few minutes later, these students made their way to one of the portable microphones set up in front of the main entrance to the building, and proudly announced to the crowd what they had done. The announcement was met with loud cheers from the protesters, who were by now blocking the entrance to the building. Knowing that this demonstration was going to take place, I had been in the building an hour before the students arrived, talking with the Professor of Military Science who was in charge of the unit. He was a combat experienced, tough, and highly intelligent Marine Corps officer. Far from fitting any stereotype the protesters had about military officers, he was cool, rational, and thoughtful. While I was quite nervous about what might become of this protest, this officer viewed it as nothing he could not handle, and joked with me about it while the protesters were pounding on the doors: "I've been in real combat, you know, and this stuff is a piece of cake compared to that!" he said.

Because I was known to many of the protesters and was viewed with at least a modicum of trust by them, I became the negotiator between the Marine Colonel and the protesters. I told the Colonel that the flag had been removed and replaced with the North Vietnam flag. While he was angry about this, he laughed and asked, "do you want me to go up there and take it down?" I had no doubts that he was fully capable of doing just that, but thought such action was unnecessary at the moment. The student protesters wanted to enter the building, and by talking with them for several minutes, I was able to hold them off. They demanded to talk directly with the Colonel, and I told them that I would ask him if he would be willing to do so, outside of the building. The students, of course, would not believe that a Marine Colonel would talk with them, so they began chanting, "we want the Colonel!" I went inside and asked the Colonel if he would talk with the large crowd. He calmly smiled, put on his officer's cap, and said to me, "sure – what do you want me to talk to them about?" I knew this Colonel did not need any advice from me!

When I brought the Colonel outside, the students were astonished, and after some nasty epithets and noisy chants filled the air, he managed to get the attention of the crowd and willingly used one of the students' portable microphones to communicate with them. It only took the Colonel about 10 minutes to disarm the students. He did not criticize them; he talked about the value of freedom of expression, the role of the military in a democracy, and about their own education at the university. After about an hour, the students had calmed down, and the Colonel was still calmly responding to questions. Even when the questions were filled with obscenities and accusations, he responded to the issue the student was raising in a respectful and thoughtful manner. By 2:30, all but about 50 of the students had dispersed. Due to the Colonel's intelligence, and his willingness to treat the students with dignity, he prevented what on some other college campus might have become a violent confrontation.

Two young male students I knew fairly well stayed around the building until about 3:00, still talking with the Colonel. They were present at most campus demonstrations against the war, but always stopped short of violating the law. After everyone else had left, these two students approached the Colonel and myself and asked if they could have our permission to take down the North Vietnamese flag on the building and return the U.S. flag to its proper place. While this did not exactly satisfy military protocol, the Colonel thanked the students and invited them into the building, where he showed them the entrance to the roof and he and I watched while they performed what had to be one of the most unusual, but touching flag raising ceremonies we had ever seen!

I had many contacts with these two students before they graduated and remained in touch with them for several years. The experience at the Naval ROTC building that afternoon in 1972 did not change their opposition to the Vietnam War, but the compassion, dignity, and respect they were shown that day by the Marine Colonel certainly was an important part of their college education.

Professors of Military Science typically are assigned to three-year terms of duty as faculty members in ROTC programs. This Marine Colonel, who moved on to an overseas assignment the next year, politely dismissed my compliments for what he did that day for the university and its students. For him, it was a piece of cake.

Confession: My Favorite Students

I was fortunate to work at universities that attracted highly talented students. It was always a pleasure seeing these gifted students excel in their academic work and to be recognized by the institution for their outstanding accomplishments. Many of them went on to graduate and professional schools and to no one's surprise, continued to succeed. Quite often, these students came from well-educated, affluent families and had the benefit of the best schools and academic support during their young lives. It was a privilege to know them as students and to see them achieve their goals.

These students were the well-known stars – the ones whose pictures were in the newspapers and the ones the university most often cited as examples of the superior graduates of the institution. They all made the university look good. While I liked and admired them, they were never my favorite students; in some ways, it seemed as if it was all too easy for them, or that the university was just one more stepping stone on their predetermined road to success.

I always preferred the underdog – the student whose parents had never been to college; the student who was not very socially polished; the student who was of average intelligence; the student who had to work to get through college; the student who was not handsome or beautiful; the student who was genuinely amazed to discover new knowledge; the student whose background would cause most people to drop out of school long before college was even a possibility. Helping and encouraging such students and seeing them overcome the odds against them gave me more satisfaction than any other aspect of my career.

Here are four examples....

Kim's mother was fortunate to escape from Vietnam in 1974 and came to Florida, where she learned English and supported herself and her two children by working long hours as a hotel maid. She had been a teacher in Vietnam. Her husband eventually was able to join her in 1979, and the family dreamed of their two children going to college. Kim excelled in her schoolwork, and was admitted to the university. By working 30 hours per week, she was able to complete her degree in pharmacy on time, despite the death of her father while she was in college. The expressions on the face of her mother and her extended family when Kim received her degree convinced me again what a powerful force education can be. Kim is now a successful pharmacist and an active leader in the alumni association.

John grew up in a small, rural town with extremely limited educational opportunities. No one in his family had completed more than eight years of school. John's father died when John was a young boy and his mother and grandparents raised him. He worked in manual labor jobs to help support his family, but fell into a rough crowd and got into trouble with the law when he was only 16, causing him to drop out of high school. One of his school counselors encouraged him to return to school and to participate in a pre-college preparation program during the summer. John entered the university in a special admissions program, but found the academic and social adjustment too daunting, failing his courses, and returning home after one year. A student affairs staff member at the university remained in touch with John and urged him to re-enroll after a year of working. John came back to the university, determined to succeed. He worked almost full time to support himself, and after five difficult, but rewarding years, he earned his degree. He is now a high school science teacher and coach, helping other young people from rough backgrounds succeed, despite the odds against them.

Sue grew up in a modest, conservative family. She went to college, earned her degree in education, and taught for four years before she and her husband had three children. She then worked as a homemaker for the next 16 years. She had always dreamed of being a veterinarian, but had never received any encouragement from anyone to pursue this option. At age 42, she decided to see what she might do to realize her dream. She discovered that she had to earn another undergraduate degree to be considered for admission to a veterinary program. Even though she lived 90 miles from the university, she commuted and completed her degree in zoology in less than three years. But, with over 400 applicants for only 80 spaces in the first year class in the veterinary medicine program, she was not admitted, despite her excellent academic record. Still determined, Sue enrolled in a Master's degree program in animal science, having been advised that completion of this degree might enhance her chances of admission to the veterinary medicine program. She continued to commute from home, fulfilling her duties there as well as working the long hours required to complete the Master's degree. Two years later, she graduated with high honors in the animal science program, and at age 47, she was admitted to the college of veterinary medicine. When she completed her D.VM degree four years later, her husband, her parents, and her three children were there as her proudest cheerleaders. By sheer determination and hard work, Sue achieved her dream, and is now in full time practice in a small animal clinic.

Bill seemed like he did not have a problem in the world while in college. He was popular, well liked, and was making good progress on his degree in business administration. He never missed a party and his friends noted that while he drank a lot, Bill always seemed in control. But in his junior year, his grades took a nosedive, and Bill rarely attended class. He flunked out of the university, but one of his faculty members was concerned about him and called a counselor, hoping to get some help for Bill. In the next two years, Bill was out of college, became addicted to both alcohol and cocaine, and became estranged from his family. The counselor at the university was able to convince Bill to enter an extended treatment program, and after a very rough year, Bill was back at the university. By participating regularly in an alcoholics anonymous program and receiving continuing counseling, Bill earned his degree, and now, 12 years later, is in a responsible position with a social service agency. He has experienced some setbacks, but he knows what he has to do to remain a healthy person, and he is determined to do this. For Bill, the support he received from the university counselor saved his life, and gave him hope. Now, his success is giving others in need some hope as well.

Yes, I confess – these underdogs were always my favorite students!